From mind to paper,
from paper to mind.

Haruko.

SPEED KINGS

Wayne Terry

First Published.
2017
Amazon Publications.

All photos are subject to copyright.
British Libraries.

All rights reserved.

BONNEVILLE SALT FLATS 1935

It's the year 1935 and a soft wind blows across the Bonneville Salt Flats in the Nevada desert under blue skies.
A tiny lizard basks in the morning sun when suddenly the ground tremors beneath it making it sprint for shelter.
In the distance is a dusty haze.
Several vehicles appear out of the dusty haze.
In amongst them all is Malcolm Campbell's Land Speed Record car called the Bluebird and its Blue aluminium body is shining in the morning sun.

TIMING TOWER

All the vehicles reach the timing officials tower and start
unloading the equipment and supplies for the record attempt.
Malcolm gets out of the Lincoln car and looks across to find his chief mechanic called Leo villa.
All the mechanics start preparing the Bluebird.

Malcolm is a tall man in his fifties with slick dark hair
combed back. He's a veteran of the First World War wearing his white overalls as he looks into the distance at the route he'll be covering.

He's joined by his son Donald, 10 who also has dark slick combed back hair wearing a brown jacket, trousers with white shirt and a blue tie. Donald looks up at his father.
"Good luck father."
Malcolm puts his arm around his son and smiles. Malcolm walks towards the team that are preparing the car for
the record attempt and try and break the 300mph barrier.
Standing in front of the Bluebird is a man called Leo Villa who is scratching his head.

Leo is a little shorter than Malcolm and has scruffy wavy black hair and is in his late twenty's, wearing white overalls.
He continues to look at the front of Bluebird.
Malcolm walks over to him. "What's wrong?"
Leo looks across at Malcolm, "I'm not happy with this set up,
She's going to get too hot; we need more air flowing through her."

Malcolm scratches his head. "That'll slow her down."
Leo looks over. "She'll be fine."
"Ok, whatever you say Leo."
The team continue to set the car up for its run.
They have with them a special machine on wheels that starts the Bluebird's Rolls Royce engine.
They wheel the machine to the side of the car and connect cables to it.
Leo checks the machine is connected up right to the car.
There are also a Dunlop tyre team checking the condition of the tyres.

Campbell walks to the side of the car, wearing his white overalls he prepares to climb into the cockpit of the Bluebird car.
He places his hands on the steering wheel and climbs onto the side of the car.
A member of the team wipes the salt off his feet and he gets into the car and grips the steering wheel nervously.
With his head down looking around the cockpit he makes his checks before giving the signal to his team to start her up.
Leo comes to the side of Bluebird and leans over to Malcolm.
"You already boss?"
Malcolm looks determined.
"Yes let's do this!"
Leo tells his team to standby and waits for Malcolm's signal.
Malcolm does his final checks inside the cockpit. Malcolm looks over towards Leo. "Ok Leo my old chum start her up!"
Leo looks at his team.
"Alright team turn her over."
They power up the portable starter that's connected to the car and it roars into life with black smoke coming out of the exhausts.
Malcolm selects first gear and pulls away towards the prepared strip of smoothed out salt.
Leo heads to the Lincoln car where Donald is waiting.
They both get in the Lincoln car and Leo starts the engine.
Donald is clutching a silver horseshoe.
Leo looks across at Donald. "What's that you got there?"
"My dad gave it to me. It's for good luck."
They speed off after Malcolm in the Bluebird.

Malcolm has almost reached the measured mile markers and is up to 110 mph changing up in the gears to get the car up to its intended speed and try and break the land speed record.
Leo with young Donald in the passenger seat of the Lincoln car gives chase.
Donald looks excited. "Come on Leo, faster!"
Leo with his foot to the floor looks over at Donald.
"This is as fast as she goes."
"Father looks great! What speed do you think he's doing?"
"Hopefully it's nearly 300mph says Leo."
"Do you really think so?"
"Yes I remember back in 1925 when he broke 150 mph in a Sunbeam he bought. I remember as if it was yesterday."

POVEY CROSS 1924

Leo and Malcolm's wife Dorothy are out in the yard at the back of Malcolm's 15th century house working on a Sunbeam 350hp racing car called Bluebird 1. Dorothy Campbell is wearing white overalls and has short brown hair and is wearing black shoes. Malcolm walks into the yard with his dog (An Alsatian cross). The dog lies down on the gravel near we're Leo is working on the car. Malcolm walks up to Leo and Dorothy and kneels down beside them looking into the engine compartment. "How's it going Leo?
"Not bad, we've managed to get an extra 10hp and will be able to use better tyres this time round. Do you still want to take her to Wales Malcolm?"
"Yes I do, I want that record Leo!"
"Ok you sure will with this monster says Dorothy."
Leo and Dorothy continue with the work on the car while Malcolm watches with anticipation.

SAN SEBASTION GRAND PRIX SPAIN 1924

A little old lady walks across a muddy road to pick up her cat which is sitting on the other side of the road licking its paws. She picks it up and hurries back to the other side to where her house is.

Suddenly a red racing car appears from round the bend followed closely by another one which is blue both traveling at speed.
The driver in the red car is Henry Segrave and behind him is a
Italian driver called Meo Costantini driving a Bugatti 35 type racing car while Henry Segrave drives a Sunbeam racing car.
Henry Segrave is wearing white overalls and a white helmet with goggles. Like Malcolm Campbell he too fought in the First World War but Henry had an injury to his hand after being shot by a German Soldier in the war but that doesn't stop his passion for racing motor cars.
He is currently in second place in the race while his team mate is first. His name is Lee Guinness and he is also racing in a red Sunbeam.
The racing cars continue racing around the tricky street circuit when Lee Guinness and his co-driver, Tom Barratt who are leading in the race suddenly have a problem.
As their car goes round one of the bends it skids on the slippery clay like service and shoots up a steep incline and stops at the top before rolling back down throwing both occupants out of the car and killing Tom Barratt and seriously wounding lee Guinness.
Henry Segrave speeds past the accident and sees his mate lee
Guinness lying at the side of the road whilst being attended by a stretcher party with no sign of his co-driver Tom Barratt to which Henry is unaware of the condition of ether men.

Henry slows the car down as he's worried that lee Guinness's
Sunbeam might have had a problem with it and assumes that he might also have a fault with his car and drives it as if it was made of glass.
Finally Henry Segrave crosses the finish line in first place with Meo Costantini in second place and a French driver called Andre Morel in third place.

Segrave pulls his car up by the stands which are full of cheering crowds and gets out of the car. He's congratulated by the officials and handed a bouquet of flowers. With a concerned look on his face Henry goes off to find out about his friends.

PENDINE SANDS WALES 1925

A year has passed and the Bluebird mechanics and the Dunlop tyre team stand around the Bluebird 1 car ready for its land speed record attempt and see if they can break the 150mph barrier. On the beach are a small number of spectators watching. Timing officials stand near the measured mile with their timing instruments ready for Captain Campbell's record attempt. One of the timing officials walks over to Malcolm. "Already to go sir?"
"Yes, just gives us a moment, we're almost ready says Malcolm."
"Ok Sir just give us a shout when you're ready."
"Will do, says Malcolm."

<u>Malcolm Campbell with the 1925 Bluebird at Pendine Sand Wales.</u>

The Bluebird team continue to prepare the car for the run while Malcolm puts his leather helmet on. Leo goes to the front of the car and inserts the starter wrench to fire up the engine. He leaves the wrench in position and comes back round to the side of the car to help the other team get her ready. Malcolm puts on his gloves.

Malcolm looks over at his team. "Ok chaps, we good to go?"
"Yes Malcolm says Leo."

Malcolm signals to the officials that he's ready for the record attempt and makes his way to the side of the car.

He climbs in and checks his instruments.

Leo goes to the front of the car and grabs the starting wrench and looks at his skipper Malcolm who is looking at his instrument panel. "Ready says Leo."

Malcolm looks at Leo. "Ok buddy start her up!"

Leo turns the starting wrench. "Contact says Malcolm."

The engine roars into life and smoke pours out of the exhausts. The team push the Bluebird away as it speeds of towards the measured mile where the officials are waiting.

The spectators are cheering as Malcolm grips the steering wheel with one hand and changes up a gear with the other as he picks up speed. The Bluebird is now doing 100mph.

Wet sand is being sprayed up around the car as it goes through the measured mile at an average speed of 147mph.

Malcolm slows the Bluebird down to turn it around to go back through the measured mile. The officials can be seen checking their timing instruments. One of the officials runs over to Malcolm who is still sitting in the Bluebird. "You have to do one more run Sir!"

Malcolm raises his goggles and looks at his tyres.

He turns to the official. "Ok says Malcolm."

He puts his accelerator down and he's away heading towards the measured mile. He slides his goggles back over his eyes and picks up speed. He flies through the measured mile at an average speed of 151mph.

"He's done it, 150.33mph, is that what you make it, screams the official as the other official looks on."

"I'll go and tell him the good news."

Malcolm slows the Bluebird down as he approaches his team.

He removes his goggles and leather helmet.

His face covered in black from the exhaust smoke.

"I think I've done it chaps! I could just make out the speed and I'm sure it's just over 150mph says Malcolm as an official runs over."

"Congratulations Sir 150.33mph. A new world record"

Malcolm puts his arms around Leo and the team.

"Well done chaps!" They start packing the car up to head back to Povey Cross.

SUNBEAM FACTORY WOLVERHAMPTON

A man wearing a suit sits behind a wooden desk.

His name is Louis Coatalen and he's one of the directors of the Sunbeam Motor Car Company.

Someone knocks on his office door. "Come in" says Louis.

Door opens and in walks Henry Segrave wearing a suit and a hat with black shoes. He approaches the desk and removes his hat.

"Ah Henry terrible news about Tom and Lee, I've informed their families."

"Looks like Lee had a lucky escape."

"How are things with you?"

Henry looks sad. "I'm ok, just a bit shocked by it all I guess but I'll be alright. I kind of feel guilty in winning the race as Lee was in the lead."
"Just think of it as a team win says Louis. Now take your jacket off and have a seat. I have a proposition for you.
The team here have been watching these land speed record attempts and we reckon we could easily develop a car that could compete and I want you to be our driver so what do you say?" Henry scratches his head.
"I don't know what to say, do you think I have enough experience, Lee is a far better driver than me and he already has a speed record at Brooklands three years ago now,
So what makes you think I could achieve one says Henry."
"You have won two Grand Prix's for Christ sake and can keep your head on the race track that's why! I'm offering you this chance take it or leave it."

"Ok can I think about it says Henry."
"Yeah sure thing, just don't take too long says Louis."
Henry grins. "I won't thank you. Now go and get some rest and I'll be in touch says Louis. "Ok thank you Mr Coatalen."
Henry puts his hat on and leaves the office.

WOLVERHAMPTON FACTORY

A group of men are working on a red racing car which is on jacks. There are spanners and other tools laid out on the work benches. Louis and Henry enter the factory and approach the car that the mechanics are working on.
"Well hear it is Henry the Sunbeam I want you to take on a beach somewhere and break the land speed record with it" says Louis.
"You think your still up for it? Yes, I'm looking forward to it. What engine is it going to have in it" replies Henry.
"It's going to have a 300hp supercharged V12 with four gears.
That's amazing it looks great so far. I can't wait to drive it."
"Do you have a place to test it?"
"We'll test it at Brooklands and hope to do the attempt at a place called Southport; it's a nice stretch of beach" replies Louis. "Ok, that sounds great, when do you think she'll be ready?"
"Hopefully sometime next summer says Louis."
"Great stuff your team has done really well."
"Thanks Henry." They continue looking around the car.

BROOKLANDS RACE TRACK

A white racing car speeds around an oval race track.
The car speeds across the start/finish line with two men standing to the side of the track.
One is wearing dark trousers a white shirt and a flat cap and is holding a clipboard.
The other man is dressed in brown trousers, white shirt and wearing a brown blazer holding a stop watch.
The racing car pulls up into the pits and a tall stocky man wearing a leather racing cap and white overalls can be seen in the racing car.
His name is Parry Thomas, an experienced racing driver and engineer. He turns the engine off and gets out of the car.

He is approached by his team who were timing him around the track. "Well! How did I do?" Says Parry.

Parry places his hands on his hips whilst clutching his dirty
gloves in his right hand. A man with a clipboard looks at Parry. "Much faster than before Parry, She's a beast!"
"I think she's ready for a record attempt, replies Parry best inform those officials."
One of Parry's team members steps forward. "Easy Parry not so fast, we've still got to sort out the overheating issues before we take her to Wales."
Parry looks frustrated. "Well best we get on with it then!
I want to at least try for the record this year."
The team roll the car towards one of the pit garages whilst
Parry looks at the clipboard.
Two German shepherd dogs are lying down by the pit wall as Parry walks towards them.

HENRY SEGRAVE RESIDENTS

A woman with long brown hair wearing a green dress is standing in a lounge of a house and places a tray with a cup and saucer with a small teapot on it down onto a coffee table.
Next to the coffee table is a man sitting in an armchair.
The man in the armchair is Henry Segrave and the woman is
Henry's wife Doris Segrave.
"I've made you some tea dear says Doris."
"Thank you Doris is there any mail?"
"No dear, there isn't." The phone starts ringing on a side cabinet. "I'll get that says Doris."
Doris goes to answer the phone which is at the other end of the lounge. She picks up the phone.
"Hello! It's for you dear."
Henry gets up out of the armchair and walk over to the phone.
Doris hands the phone over to Henry.
"Hello, Henry here!"
On the other end of the phone is Louis Coatalen.
"Hi Henry how have you been keeping? Ok thank you, how are things? All good says Henry." We've almost got the V12 Sunbeam ready and we'll be taking her to a stretch of beach at Southport." Just wanted to check if you're still up to driving her Henry? Of course when?"
"I'll call you replies Louis."
"I hear you're having problems with the supercharger?"
"Yes but we've almost sorted it. It'll be fixed for the run I promise Henry."
"Ok, I'll look forward to it says Henry."
"Ok bye replies Louis."
Henry places the handset back down and turns to his wife who is standing behind him. "What's wrong with the supercharger?"
"Nothing dear everything will be fine."
He kisses his wife on the forehead.

SOUTHPORT BEACH

Crowds of people gather around a lorry on Southport beach.
The lorry is carrying a racing car covered by a sheet.

A man climbs up onto the back of the lorry and pulls the sheet
off the car. They unload the car onto the beach and set it up for the record attempt.
The car is a red Sunbeam V12 with superchargers fitted to it.
The Earl of Cottenham and Leyland motors Engineer/racing driver Parry Thomas is looking on.

Henry Segrave is talking to Louis Coatalen. Henry is wearing his white overalls and a dark helmet as he discusses to Louis about the car, Parry walks over to greet him. "Morning Henry, just want to wish you good luck." He shakes Henry's hand whilst looking at the car.
"She looks a beast; do you reckon she'll beat the record?"
Henry is feeling confident. "I hope so, thank you."
Parry walks off towards the crowd that has gathered while Henry gets ready for the run. Henry speaks to his mechanic.
"Do you think the superchargers are going to hold out?"
"I'm not sure Henry, They should do!"
Henry does his helmet strap up and prepares to climb into the car. Louis walks up to Henry and places his hand on Henry's shoulder. "You ready Henry?" Yes I think so!"
"Henry listen to me, if those supercharger's pack up I want you to keep going."
"Ok I will, just make sure you have the fire engine on standby in case she catch's fire. Will do good luck!"
The team start the engine and give the thumbs up to the timing
officials that there ready for the attempt.
"Ok away you go says one of the officials."

The team spread themselves either side of the rear of the car and all push the red Sunbeam. It roars off into the distance towards the measured mile.
Henry struggling to keep the car straight grips the steering wheel while he gets up to speed.
The supercharger's kick in and the car goes through the measured mile.

<u>Henry Segrave with the Red Sunbeam on Ainsdale Beach Southport.</u>

Henry slows the car down to turn it around for his return run.
Smoke pours out the exhausts as he turns the car around.
He speeds off again heading in a northerly direction.
Suddenly at about 150mph the car hits a bump in the sand and launches the sunbeam in the air just a few inches off the ground which makes the engine race and blows the superchargers. As the car lands back on the sand Henry keeps the car going and flies through the measured mile at a speed of 153mph.

Henry knows he's beating the record and taps the side of the car as he makes his way back to his team. As he approach's he slows the car down and turns the engine off as the team swarm around the car cheering.
"You've done it Henry says one of his team."

The team lift Henry from out of the car and carry him away cheering with Henry putting his hands up in the air.
The Sunbeam car is in the background with smoke coming out of the vents but is not on fire. The team head off towards the hotel to celebrate.

POVEY CROSS

Malcolm is sitting in his armchair reading a newspaper at his house when suddenly he slams it down on the coffee table.
"Damn it" shouts Malcolm. Dorothy and the dog come in the room. "What's wrong" asks Dorothy.
"That bloody Segrave has only gone and taking the record from me."
"Let me see!"
Dorothy picks up the paper when Leo walks in the room.
"I've finished changing the plugs on that car, what's up?"
"Henry Segrave has beating Malcolm's record" says Dorothy.
She hands the paper to Leo who reads it.
"Well it was only a matter of time I guess" replies Leo.
Malcolm sighs. "Leo's right, what are you going to do honey?"
"I'm going to take it back! I've already been in touch with Amherst Villiers about using one of their new Napier aero engines. I've arranged to see him next month."
Leo sits down. "I didn't hear about this, why didn't you tell me?"
"You were too busy getting the racing car ready for the next race old chum." Dorothy hands a coffee to Leo.
"When we get to the British Grand Prix, I'm hoping that Amherst and his team will be developing a new car for me.
Well that's great news Malcolm. Yes and I'll need you to fine tune it for me, the usual stuff."
Leo and Malcolm drink there coffee's while Dorothy leaves the lounge. "Once Amherst finishes with the plans for the car I'm going to try and build it hear so I need your help more than ever. Basically I want you to oversee the construction of the car." Malcolm continues. "I'm going to be adding to the team,

I've got a few new mechanics joining us." I've got George and Charles Miller of Robinhood Engineering being supervised by Joseph Maina, they all come highly recommended."
"Well that's great!" Replies Leo.

"Yes it is that's why we need to make room in the garage so we can get started once Amherst has done the drawings and the new team arrive in a couple of weeks. The only problem at the moment is I haven't told Dorothy." Leo laughs to himself.
"Good luck with that. "Right best go over this Bugatti as we haven't got long for the next race."

Leo puts his cup down on the coffee table and stands up to leave the lounge. As he gets to the door Malcolm stands up and calls Leo. "Leo I really appreciate all you've done for me, I've couldn't of done it without you mate."
"That's okay, don't mention it."
Leo leaves the room and Malcolm sits back down and pats the dog as he goes to drink his coffee.

PENDINE SANDS WALES APRIL 1926

A white racing car with Babs written on the side sits on a wet beach facing north with an empty cockpit. Parry Thomas is standing to the rear of Babs.

Parry is wearing a white polo neck sweater with a dark jacket over it and dark trousers with black shoes.
He puts on his helmet and prepares to climb into Babs.
His team, wearing white polo neck jumpers with Dunlop stitched on the front prepare the racing car. There are timing officials standing near the measured mile all wearing white overcoats. The timing officials give the thumbs up to show their timing equipment is ready.

Parry Thomas in Babs before his record breaking run at Pendine.

Parry climbs into the cockpit of Babs and the team start Babs up. Babs roars into live. One of the team member runs to the side of Babs and shouts to Parry.
"All set to go Parry?"
Parry has to shout over the noise of the V12 engine.
"Yes, let's go!" Parry pulls his goggles over his eyes and the team get to the back of Babs and start pushing the car.
Parry selects first gear and he's away. With the back wheels skidding he gets up to speed and heads towards the measured mile.
Gripping the steering wheel he lowers his head behind the windscreen and goes ever faster as he flies through the measured mile which is being indicated by flags in the sand.
With sand spraying up in his goggles and around the car he tries to slow it down so he can turn Baps around for its return run.

He skids the car to the left slightly but manages to control it and slowly turns the car around to start his return run.
He puts his foot down on the accelerator as he changes up a gear and slowly picks up speed. He races towards the measured mile gripping the steering wheel hard, faster and ever faster as he flies past the flags with the engine roaring and wet sand spraying all over the car and Parry's face. With an average speed of 170mph he has done it.
Parry wipes his goggles and face as he tries to slow the car down. He goes down in the gears to try and help the car slow down as the brakes are overheating and smoke comes out of them. He manages to slow her down and heads towards his team who run towards him carrying their equipment and a fire extinguisher.

As he slows down the team swarm around the car.
The car finally stops and Parry turns off the engine.
Parry looks exhausted as his team help him out of the car.
He takes his goggles and his helmet off as he puts his arm around one of his team members.
"What was my speed? I must have broken the record!"
"You have boss! We've just got to wait for the official timings from the Marshall's says a team member."

Timing official runs over with a piece of paper in his hand and approach's Parry and the team by which time local spectators have gathered around the car and the team with Parry in the middle of them all.
"Your speed Sir was 171.02mph a new land speed record, congratulations!" Says the official.
He hands the piece of paper to Parry's team as they lift Parry
up in the air on their shoulders. Everyone cheers
They try to carry Parry through the crowd of cheering people
towards the hotel there staying in but the crowd are wild
because of Parry being Welsh, they just love him.
Some reporters manage to rush up to Parry who now has been put
down off the teams shoulders.
"How does it feel Parry to be a record breaker?" Says the reporter. "It feels great, I'm very pleased for the team, they've worked really hard on this car, I'm very proud of them replies Parry."
"You've achieved an incredible speed of over 170mph, beating the likes of Segrave and Campbell, you must be very pleased."
"Yes I'm very pleased, thank you." Parry and his team head off towards the hotel.

INDIANAPOLIS MAY 1926

Rain is pouring down on thousands of spectators all sitting around a huge oval racetrack. There are 13 racing cars left on the track out of the 28 starters and at the front is a young driver called Frank Lockhart who driving for the Harry Millers team, his car is white and has the number 15 written on the side.
It is the 158th lap out of 160 and it's still raining.
The race has already been stopped once and looks like it could be stopped again as the drivers try to keep their racing cars on the track. In the middle of the track is the pit lane where all the pit crews are anxiously watching their driver's race as they try and keep their cars from sliding off the track.
In one of the pit lanes is Frank's team boss called Harry
Miller who is standing with Frank's wife and her name is Ella.
They are both holding an umbrella. Harry shouts out as Frank speeds by. "Come on Frank, bring it home!" He turns to Ella.
"What a driver, you're a lucky girl to be married to that kid sweetheart! I know he's amazing" replies Ella.
They continue watching the cars race around the track when the
rain gets harder. On the track Frank is fighting hard to keep his place as another driver is trying to take over him.
The other driver is an American like Frank and his name is Dave Lewis. Suddenly Dave's car has a problem as he tries to take the inside lane, his engine starts smoking and he has to pull into the pits and retire. Frank now has a commanding lead from all the other remaining cars behind as he fights to keep the car from sliding in the wet.
Suddenly because of the rain a man is seen running onto the track and is seen waving a chequered flag. The race is over and Frank has won the race at the young age of 24, the youngest to win the Indianapolis 500.
The spectators stand up cheering as Frank waves at them as he drives by on his way back to the pits.
In the pit lane Ella, Harry and the rest of the Miller race team can be seen cheering and shouting."
Fantastic what a race!" Frank arrives at his team's lane and stops the car.
A group of journalist's carrying cameras can be seen rushing towards Frank and the team.
Ella rushes over and hugs Frank while he's still sitting in the car. Harry walks over to Frank.

"Well done kid, how would you like to race for me on a permanent basis?" Harry expects Frank will be over the moon to be asked but to Harry's shock Frank replies. "No thank you Harry, I'll have to pass but I'd would like to buy the racing car!"
He taps the side of the car as he climbs out of it and puts his arm around his wife. Harry looks shocked that Frank turned down the offer as Frank is blocked by photographers as he tries to go and collect his reward money. Frank turns to Harry. "Well, can I buy the car off you?"
Harry scratches his head whilst looking at the car. "Sure why not!" Frank shakes his hand. "I'll come and see you tomorrow and sort it out ok" says Frank. "Sure thing kid."
Frank turns to the press that are crowding him and his wife.
"Congratulations on your win Frank will you be entering the next races?" says the reporter Frank runs his hands through his greasy hair. "Yes I will be, hope to win them too."
Frank smiles with his wife.
"Well best of luck" replies the reporter.
Frank smiles and waves as he and his wife make their way through the crowd to collect their winnings.

BROOKLANDS AUGUST 1926

Its race day at Brooklands and crowds are cheering in the stands along the pit straight.
Racing cars are lined up on the start/finish line.
Some racing drivers are sitting in their cars while others are standing by them while their mechanics prepare them.
The line-up consisted of four British drivers and about seven French drivers. The British drivers were Malcolm Campbell, Henry Segrave, F Halford and G Eyston. As for the French drivers you had the likes of Robert Benoist, Albert Divo, Robert Senechal, Louis Wagner and Jules Moriceau to name but a few.

There also is a mix of racing car makes on the track such as
Aston Martin's, Talbot 700's, Delage 155B's and a Bugatti 39A driven by Malcolm Campbell.
All the racing cars had different performances but the fastest on the track were the Talbot 700's which one of them was driven by ace driver Henry Segrave.
Henry's wife is standing next to his car no 9.

In front of Henry is Jules Moriceau and his car no 6 also a
Talbot 700. Behind Henry is Malcolm's car no 7.
On the front row of the grid are the two French drivers and their mechanics sitting in their cars no's 14 and no 2.

Both racing cars are two seater Delage 155B's. All the other racing cars are single seater's. Malcolm is putting on his leather helmet whilst standing by his car as Leo supervisor's the team. Leo looks towards Malcolm.
"I take it you know who's in front of you boss?" Yes Leo, I have noticed." Leo laughs. "Aren't you going to wish him well?
"Certainly not replies Malcolm."
Leo continues to chuckle to himself and the team.
Henry is still working on his car with his team.
He picks up an old rag and wipes his hands on it whilst looking back down the grid. An announcer is heard over the large speakers. "Two minutes to start!"
The crowd roar with excitement. Doris Segrave walks up to Henry as he prepares to get in his racing car.
"Be careful" says Doris looking concerned.
Henry smiles and kisses his wife and Doris goes off to the pits. Henry gets in his car and turns to his team.
"This car may be fast but I'm not happy with the brakes or the rest of the set-up, how many laps do you think she'll do?"

"Not sure, but we've done everything we can for her just take it easy with her" replies the mechanic.
Henry's mechanic has a final inspection of the car by walking around it and walks back to Henry.
"Good luck Henry."
Henry acknowledges his team mate by giving him the thumbs up as he puts his gloves on. The rest of the other drivers are in their cars ready to go.
A man walks onto the track in front of the cars and signals to the drivers to start their engines. A roar goes out across the stands as the loud engines start up.
The drivers start revving their engines as the man standing in front of them holds a flag and prepares to wave it.
Malcolm grips his steering wheel and selects first gear.

Man with the flag moves to the side of the racetrack and lowers the flag to the ground. The racing cars speed off the starting line and the crowd cheer. All the drivers jostle for position as they approach the first bend with Malcolm shooting past Segrave as Segrave has to apply the brakes early due to his cars speed. As Malcolm shoots past Segrave narrowly misses Moriceau whose axle has just broken on his red Talbot 700 and comes to a stop by the safety fence with all the other cars rushing by him.

The drivers in front (Senechal/Benoist) are battling with each other for first place and don't see Malcolm speeding past them on the outside of the track.
Malcolm is now in first position as he completes his first lap. As Malcolm races across the start/finish line Leo can be seen with his team leaning over the pit wall cheering his skipper on as Malcolm and all the other cars chasing him speed past and continue around the circuit.

POVEY CROSS

Malcolm Campbell's garage has one of its doors partly open.
Inside the garage men are working on what looks like a chassis of a car. It is long with a large engine close to the centre of the chassis just in front of a steering wheel with large four wheels fitted to it.
The men working on the car come from a company called Robinhood Engineering Works (KLG).
They now work for Malcolm Campbell.
Their names are George and Charles Miller and they are being helped by two metal panel beaters from a company called Jarvis Coach Builders and an engine specialist from the Napier Company called Joe Coe.
They've all been working hard on Malcolm's new Bluebird and there almost finished. Dorothy walks into the garage carrying a tray with coffee/tea and biscuits on it.
Dorothy puts the tray down on one of the work benches.
"Here you go boys!"
"Thanks Mrs Campbell" says George.
Dorothy looks on as the men continue to work on the car.
Charles stands with his hands on his waist. "Do you really think the chassis is going to take the weight of the engine at over 150mph George?" says Charles.
"Sure it will now pass me that 19mm wrench and stop being negative, your starting to worry me." The rest of the team laugh. "Anyway what are the odds on the boss finishing first at Brooklands, Joe?" says George.
Joe wipes his hands with an old rag and picks up a cup of
coffee with his other and looks towards George.
"I don't know about you but I reckon he'll get second says Joe. "That so ehh, I reckon it'll be 1st, with that Bugatti he's driving, boy what a machine" says George.
"Then I'll say third cos it's not as fast as those Talbots" replies Charles. The team laugh and throw there oil rags at Charles.

BROOKLANDS LAP 60

Malcolm is still leading the race with Senechal hot on his tail while Benoist comes into the pits. In fifth place is Henry but there's a problem with his car when his supercharger fails and he has to come into the pits.
Now Campbell has a good lead hoping his car will make it the full 110 lap's now only 50 laps to do.
Segrave arrives in the pits, looking dirty and exhausted he
climbs out of his red Talbot and heads straight to the engine.
His team are there with him looking at the engines supercharger. "It looks shot Henry says his mechanic."
"Do we have any spares" replies Segrave.
"I'm afraid not that's it there's nothing we can do Henry."
On the track Malcolm is still in the lead. As Malcolm goes around the Byfleet Banking his rear tyre blows out. He struggles to keep the car straight as he tries to get the car back to the pits.
In the pits Malcolm reaches his team with the burst tyre.
His team jump into action and have a jack ready for the car as
Malcolm gets out the car and stands with his arms folded while one man jacks the car up and the rest of the team hurry changing the wheel. Malcolm keeps an eye on what's going on. He encourages his team to hurry. "Come on chaps faster!"

The team finish putting a new rear wheel on the car and Malcolm jumps back in the car, starts the engine and heads back out onto the track only to find he's now in third place and puts his foot down to try and catch up to the racing car in front of him in second place.
There's only four cars left in the race when suddenly the
driver in fourth place has a problem. Its Albert Divo's Talbot, his supercharger has failed the same that happened to Henry's Talbot. Albert takes his strickerned car to the pits while the other three racing cars continue round the track.
Malcolm continues to chase the two cars in front when Robert
Benoist has to pull into the pits. Malcolm is now in second place. In the pits Robert is helped out of his car as the exhaust has over heated his feet and the team put his feet in a bowl of cool water. "Give him a minute to cool down and get him back in the car Andre. You'll be alright to drive as there are only two laps left" says team member.
Andre moves round to the driver's side and gets in the car while the team help Robert back in the car.
"Ok we all set?" Let's go" says the team member.
They push the car away as the engine kicks in and Andre drives the car back on the track. Malcolm gets ever closer to the leading car but it's not enough as a man appears on the track waving a chequered flag. The race is over and the crowds in the stands cheer.

Robert and Louis are first with Malcolm in second and Robert and Andre in third. They all drive into the pits.
The media rush towards Robert and Louis who are getting out of their racing car while Malcolm gets out of his car and looks on. Leo runs up to Malcolm.
"Not bad boss, almost ehh." Malcolm is worn out and disappointed whilst supporting himself against his racing car.
Malcolm wipes his face with a rag and smiles at Leo. Malcolm and Leo go off to go and get a drink while the rest of the team sort out the racing car ready for the trip back to Povey Cross.

SUNBEAM FACTORY JANUARY 1927

Sunbeam factory is busy with engineers working on a new car for the next land speed record attempt designed by Mr Irving.

There is no body on the car just the chassis with two aero engines fitted to it at either end and has power cables running from it. The whole chassis is raised off the factory floor by stands. There are no wheels fitted to it yet as they are still being developed by the Dunlop tyre company.
Mr Coatalen and Henry Segrave appear on the factory floor and walk up to the engineers working on the car.
"Well here she is Henry. What do you think?"
Henry looks up in amazement at the size of the car.
"Well I'm impressed, what's the horse power of the engines again?"
"Jack is saying they develop 400hp each and once there torqued up they'll produce about 900hp" says Louis.
"900! Wow, that's quite a lot." Henry's still amazed looking on he moves closer to the car and touches the chassis.
"Yes it is we reckon she'll break 200mph" says Louis.
"Surely you're not expecting her to do that at Southport beach. Surely we need a longer beach" replies Henry?
"Yes we know that. We found a good location for her in America."
"Where in America" says Henry?
"A long stretch of beach on the east coast of America called Daytona Beach" replies Louis.
"How soon before she's ready?"
"Should be in the next couple of months providing the tyres are ready from Dunlop" replies Louis.
"That's great stuff. They both continue looking at the car.

BROOKLANDS RACETRACK

Two German Shepard dogs are lying down on a garage floor with
Parry Thomas's land speed car (Babs) jacked up on stands with an oil tray under it.
Parry walks into the garage with one of his mechanics.
"We've done everything you've asked and I reckon you'll get an extra 12hp out of her." Parry carrying a hanky is nursing a cold. He blows his nose and goes to inspect the car.
"12hp you say. Is she still stable?" says Parry.
"Yes of course" replies the mechanic.
"What do you think her top speed will be now?" says Parry
"With the right conditions, I'd say at least 180mph."
Parry walks over to his dogs still lying on the floor and pats them both, they start panting. Parry snuffles and wipes his nose. "Good, you've all done a good job, well done!"
Parry walks out the garage with his dogs.

POVEY CROSS

Outside the garage Malcolm is standing with his hands on his hips watching his team wheel out the new Napier Bluebird.
"Nice and easy lads" he says. Leo approach's Malcolm.
"Ok she's ready. When do you want to take her to Pendine?"
"Next week we'll do it" replies Malcolm.
"Ok I'll inform the official's" says Leo.
"Great stuff Leo. Let's hope the weathers alright."

PENDINE SANDS 4TH FEB

Malcolm's team is waiting on the wet beach. In the distance Malcolm appears in the new Bluebird driving down a concrete slope onto the beach. He drives towards his team and pulls up alongside them. "How's she running?" says Leo.
Malcolm gives the thumbs up. "She's great" replies Malcolm.
Leo and the team make a final check of the car before the run.

"Tyres good?" says Leo to the team. The Dunlop team that are there check the tyres. "They look good" replies the Dunlop team. They signal to the timing officials that there ready to go and send Malcolm driving the Bluebird off on its run.
The car gets faster and faster when suddenly the rear tyre blows and he stops short at the timing line. The timing officials rush to see if he is alright.
"Are you ok Mr Campbell?" Malcolm raises his goggles and wipes his face. "Yes I'm fine dam tyre blew" he says.
Malcolm's team arrive exhausted from running almost the length of the beach check to see the damaged tyre.
It's only gone and damaged the axle; we'll have to take her back to the garage. Malcolm hits the side of the car.
By now a small gathering of spectators are surrounding the team and the car. In among them is Parry Thomas who is looking on with interest. Parry leans over towards Malcolm who's still sitting in the car while the team try to push the car onto wooden boards to stop the Bluebird sinking in the wet sand.
"Having a bit of trouble there I see Malcolm?" says Parry.
Malcolm sinks himself into the cockpit and tries to ignore him whilst his team push the car onto the wooden boards.
Malcolm gets out the car and they manage to load it up onto a lorry. Malcolm and the team get in a car and head off to the hotel there staying in while the Bluebird is taken to the garage for repairs.

The next day the Bluebird is back on the beach and the team have fixed the suspected rear broken axle caused by the tyre blowing. Malcolm prepares to get into the cockpit of the Bluebird. "I try and take it steady with her this time. I'll try not to push her to hard."

They start the Napier engine and Malcolm gets underway gradually picking up speed he flies through the measured mile.
At an average first run speed of 172mph he slows the car down to turn it around for another run.
Malcolm gets the Bluebird back up to speed and floors it through the measured mile at an average speed of 175mph.
This time the tyres stay intact and he drives up to his team who are waiting anxiously. As Malcolm slows down Leo and the team run up to him. "I think you've done it Malcolm."

Malcolm with the Napier Bluebird 1927.

They wait for confirmation from the timing officials.
A timing official runs over with a piece of paper in his hands and hands it to Malcolm who's still sitting in the car.
"Congratulations Sir, a speed of 174.224, a new land speed record."
The team start cheering as they help Malcolm out of the Bluebird. Malcolm looks exhausted but relieved he's taking back the record and is carried off by his team.

WOLVERHAMPTON SUNBEAM FACTORY

A team of mechanics can be seen outside the Sunbeam Factory pushing a large vehicle into the side entrance of the factory.
It has a large sheet over it as it's pushed into the factory where Louis, Jack and Henry are waiting.
They all gather around the large vehicle that's covered by a sheet when one of the assistant mechanics pulls the sheet off to reveal a large red streamlined body with large black wheels. The car there all looking at is the 1000hp Sunbeam.
"Well Henry she's ready. What do you think?"
She's a beast alright."

"A beast that's going to be travelling at over 200mph and you'll be the one controlling it Henry" says Jack.
Henry stands there looking at it in amazement.
"It'll be an honour, thank you." They all continue looking at the car.

PENDINE SANDS 3RD MARCH

Parry Thomas stands next to his car (Babs) and looks ahead in the distance while putting his leather helmet on.
A small crowd of people can be seen gathered by the car.
The team can be seen preparing the car for its run.

Parry prepares himself whilst coughing and sneezing.
One of the team members walks over to Parry carrying his goggles and gloves.
"Are you sure Parry you should be doing this attempt today in your state, perhaps we can wait till tomorrow?"
Parry snatches the goggles and gloves out of his hands.
"Don't tell me what I should and shouldn't do, I'm fine!"

They continue preparing the car while Parry climbs into the cockpit and puts on his goggles and gloves and checks his instruments. "Ok let's start her up!" says Parry.
The team crank the aero engine and it fires into life. The team move out of the way while Parry puts it into gear and the car moves off along the beach. As Parry picks up speed the team can see that he's struggling to keep the car straight.
"He shouldn't be driving in his condition," says one of his team members.
"You can't tell him, he just won't listen," says the other.
"Looks like he's doing a good speed, I reckon he just might pull it off." Parry flies through the measured mile whilst fighting to keep Babs in a straight line, he slows the car down to turn her around and head back towards the measured mile. He gets up to speed and pushes the accelerator pedal further and goes ever faster when suddenly on Parry's right side where the chain is it suddenly snaps and swings wildly and strikes Parry in the head killing him instantly. He let's go of the wheel which causes the car to swerve and flip over several times and finally rests upright.

The team are all horrified on what they've just witnessed.
"Come on hurry John call the ambulance over!"
They run over to the wreckage of Babs to find a lifeless body of Parry Thomas slumped over the steering wheel.
The team pull Parry out and away from the smouldering car while the fire team douse Babs in foam to stop her from catching fire while Parry's body is carried away.
The team decide to bury the car where it landed. They start burying the car with sand.

The wreckage of Babs that took Parry Thomas's life at Pendine Beach.

Some of the team check on the ambulance crews who now have put the lifeless body of Parry into the ambulance "There's nothing we can do we're very sorry" says the ambulance crew member. The team bow their heads.
"Ok we'll inform his family." The ambulance takes the body away while the team head back to the hotel looking shocked and upset.

BEREGARIA LINER NORTH ATLANTIC

A man stands on the top balcony of a luxury cruise liner looking out to sea wearing a dark suit and a Panama hat.
It is Henry Segrave and he's traveling with his wife to America to take back the land speed record with the 1000hp Sunbeam. Henry stands with his right hand in his suit pocket and his left hand resting on the ships railings.
Along the balcony can be seen two men walking towards him.
Both of the men are also wearing suits and wearing hats.
They are Louis Coatalen and Jack Irving.

They both stop along the balcony and look towards Henry from a distance.
"Do you think he's having second thoughts?" says Louis.
"No, he's probably shocked that the time has finely arrived and he's very lucky and honoured to be doing this."
"Well I don't know about you or Henry, but I'm dead nervous that we can pull this off, 200mph is a big gamble we're taking, you sure we can achieve that speed Jack?"
"Of Cause, stop worrying."
They are both interrupted by one of the ships staff.
"Sorry to disturb you gentlemen, I have a message for Mr Coatalen."
He hands a strip of paper to Louis and walks away.
Louis reads the message; shock appears on his face as he reads the message. "What is it Louis?"
"It's about that racing driver who lives at Brooklands racetrack." What about him?" replies Jack. Louis looks up at Jack. "He's dead; he's been killed trying to take back the land speed record at Pendine sands a few weeks ago.
"What happened?" says Jack. "It says here his chain broke and hit him in the side of the head killing him instantly."
"Jesus Christ!" says Jack with a look of shock on his face.
Jack takes his hat off and walks to the side railings of the ship and scratches his head. "I don't think Henry needs to know, do you?" Jack turns to Louis.
"You can't keep that from him Louis, he'll need to know."
Henry walks up behind Louis. "Need to know what?"
Louis turns round to face Henry and hands him the strip of paper.

"We thought it's not what you want to know considering you're going to be doing exactly what he was doing."
Henry is reading the message and looks up at Louis.
"You don't have to do the attempt Henry if you don't want too."
"You think that this will stop me from getting in that monster of a machine that you and Jack have created and take back the record, you must be mistaking because nothing will stop me from taking that record back."
"Ok, I'm glad to hear it Henry." He hands the message back to Louis. "Parry knows the risks, we all do, right I'll be in my cabin with Doris if you need me," replies Henry.
Jack looks at Louis while Henry walks away. "What?"
You know, I can't believe you we're suggesting not to tell him" says Jack. Louis shrugs his shoulders and they both walk off together.

NAPIER WORKS ASTON

A group of men can be seen standing around a seaplane with no wings attached to it. There discussing what needs to be done.
A man in the middle of the group is wearing a hat and a suit and is speaking to the group while pointing at the plane.
The man's name is Montagu Stanley Napier, head of Napier
Engines and is a very old man and standing next to him in the group is Chief Designer Reginald "Rex" Pierson.
Malcolm Campbell, Leo villa and the rest of the team are also there and will be working in the corner of the Napier Works

Factory building a new Bluebird with Mr Napier, Mr Pierson and their team and will be using the 900 hp aero engine that has to be removed from the seaplane that there all looking at.
Malcolm walks over to a bench with Reginald which has a drawing on it of what the Bluebird will look like when it's finished.
Malcolm nods as Reginald explains the drawing to him.
The rest of the team start stripping out the aero engine from
the seaplane.

NEW YORK DOCKS

Thousands of cheering New Yorkers are at the docks as they all wait to see Henry Segrave and his wife coming of the ship that has just docked.
Henry appears with his wife at the walk ramp and waves to the crowd Doris smiling at her husband seems overwhelmed by it all. The next day we all start to make the journey down to Daytona with Jack and Louis in the lead car and Henry and Doris driving behind.

There are several other cars making the trip with us.
It will take us several hours to get down to Daytona.
The sun is shining, it's warm and the windows are down on Henry's car. Doris puts her right arm out the window.
Wind is blowing in her hair
"Whooo hooo!" shouts out Doris. All the cars are traveling south on the highway at about 70mph.
Up ahead in the distance the police have blocked the road.
Henry and the others stop by the police road block thinking that they were in trouble for speeding.
Henry turns to his wife.
"Stay in the car honey, I won't be long."
Henry gets out of the car and is joined by Louis and they both walk towards the road block. A policeman approach's them.
He is the chief of police for Daytona and shakes Henry's hand.
Mr Segrave I take it! We've been instructed to escort you to Daytona Sir." The police have motorcycles that ride ever side of the long line of cars towards Daytona.
They all reach Daytona and are greeted by the Mayor of Daytona then are taken to their hotels.

DAYTONA BEACH 29TH MARCH 1927

A week has passed and everyone is on Daytona Beach. They prepare the Sunbeam Mystery for its runs. Henry looks nervous.
He stands next to the Sunbeam putting his gloves on while the team set up the car. Henry's wife looks on anxiously.

Henry Segrave rests before his attempt to hit 200mph at Daytona.

Henry climbs into the Sunbeam and gives the all clear for his team to start her up. The car roars into live as smoke can be seen coming out of the exhausts. Spectators start cheering.
Henry puts the car into first gear and sets off on his first run at low speed.
Everything is fine so he drives through the timing markers to check that there working and the timing officials can be seen acknowledging to Henry that there timing instruments are working fine as he slows the car down to turn her around and make the attempt on the record.

Henry is heading from North to South along the flat beach.
He picks up speed, the car now doing 150mph going ever faster he flies through the measured mile averaging 205mph. He slows the car down at the southern end of the beach ready for his final return run. As he tries to slow the car down the car is going from side to side as Henry fights with the car to keep it straight.
He comes to a stop as part of his team start changing the tyres. The brakes can be seen smoking. They finish changing the tyres and Henry is underway again now going from South to North going faster and faster as he approaches the timing markers. He flies through the timing markers.
Doris can be seen holding her hands over her mouth hoping the
Sunbeam stays its course. Henry goes to slow the car down but the brake pads are worn and he selects a lower gear and puts the Sunbeam partly in the sea to slow her down. As the Sunbeam slows down Henry manages to turn the car around and head back towards his team. His team look relieved that he is okay as they see him having to put the car in the sea to slow it down.

The team rush around the car as it comes to a stop. Henry cuts the two aero engines and is helped out of the car as the press rush over.
The police try to form a cordon around the car to keep the press at bay as Henry gets his breath back after the fast speed that he has just endured. Doris rushes over with Louis and gives Henry a kiss and a cuddle while Louis looks very pleased with what Henry has just achieved. Louis shakes Henry's hand.
"Henry, well done my boy, I'm sure you've broken the 200mph barrier, well done" says Louis.

Henry still with his arm around his wife looking exhausted but relieved smiles at Louis. "Thank you boss, what a machine she is!" A timing official squeezes through the crowd of press to reach Henry and his team to hand him a slip of paper with the speed on it. Louis takes the slip of paper off the official and starts to read it. Jack is standing next to Louis. "Well Louis what was it?"
"203.79mph a new world record!"
Everyone starts cheering as the team hoist Henry up on their shoulders. The press frantically try to get a photograph as the team carry Henry away. Jack can be seen walking next to Doris. "I told you he'd be ok." Doris smiles. "Thank you Jack for all you've done." I really appreciate it, thanks" says Henry as they all head off back to the hotel.

NAPIERS FACTORY

Leo and the Napier team continue to work on the new Bluebird car. The car is up on stands with tools and parts dotted around it while the team are tightening nuts and bolts.
Malcolm Campbell enters the workshop with another man dressed in black wearing a black top hat. His name is Lord Wakefield and has taking a fine interest in breaking land speed records. There both walk up to the team working on the car. Malcolm points to the engine area.
"Well here it is and this is the mighty Napier engine that's going to power it and hopefully take her past 200mph."
"We've certainly come a long way with the amount of horse power that these engines can now produce, it looks fantastic Malcolm."
"Yes I know, the lads have done a great job and I don't know what I'd do without them" says Malcolm looking proud.
"How soon do you think it'll be ready for the attempt?"
"Hopefully next month" says Malcolm.

"Well I wish you all the best." I'm thinking of awarding a trophy and a cheque for £1000 for every new record that's made, what do you think of that?"
"That sounds great Sir" says Malcolm. They both leave the workshop while the team continue to work on the Bluebird.

BROOKLANDS RACETRACK

Crowds are standing ever side of a racetrack.
They are waiting for Henry Segrave driving the Sunbeam Mystery that broke the 200mph barrier on Daytona Beach.
Henry is doing a victory lap on the circuit in front of thousands of cheering spectators and press.

Henry roars past the cheering crowd as the Sunbeam banks around the track. He makes his way into the pits where the police have set up a cordon. He drives into the cordon as hundreds of spectators and press run towards him. Doris, Louis, Jack and the rest of the Sunbeam team are all inside the cordon and greet Henry.

By now the crowd have surrounded the car and the team and are kept back by the cordon that the police have set up.

Henry revs the car a couple of times to the delight of the crowd who all cheer. He then turns it off and is helped out of the car. He reaches over to his wife who is standing close by wearing a hat and they kiss. Henry rubs Doris's arms.
"You ok my dear?" says Henry.
"Yes I'm fine darling."
Henry walks over to the press with Jack and Louis.
A reporter places a microphone in front of Henry. "Congratulations on your record Sir, have you heard that your rival Malcolm is building a new Bluebird and that he wants to race it against your Sunbeam?"
"Yes I've heard this but I will not be racing him instead we hope to develop a new car to take the record back if he takes the record off us," replies Henry.
"When will we be able to see this new car?"
Henry turns to Jack Irvine. Jack leans forward.
"Not for a while yet as it's not even come off the drawing board, it'll be several months before it goes into production, you'll just have to wait and see Henry." Doris and the team head off and go into a building.

NAPIER FACTORY

Leo walks over to his team who are finishing off preparing the Bluebird for shipment to Daytona.
"Make sure everything is secure on her before she gets crated up." says Leo.
Malcolm appears carrying a newspaper and walks over to Leo who is inspecting the car. "Have you seen this Leo, my old chum?
"No, what is it?" Says Leo. Malcolm hands the paper to Leo.
"It's Segrave showing off that Sunbeam of his round Brooklands, I just hope we can beat his record" says Malcolm.
"Of course we will, have faith skipper." Malcolm places his hands on his hips while watching the team preparing the car for transit to the States. "Ummm I hope so" says Malcolm.

GARAGE DAYTONA 1928

Malcolm and the team have unloaded the Bluebird and are working on the car that is in a garage they are using.
Malcolm is standing next to Leo as the team are working.
Two men walk into the garage and walk up to Leo and Malcolm.
They are both representatives of the Mayor of Daytona and are both dressed in grey suits and wearing hats.
"Good evening Mr Campbell, I have an invitation for you to attend a club in the town from the Mayor, he would like you to meet someone by the name of Mr Lockhart, perhaps you've heard of him?"
Malcolm takes the invitation from him.
"I have indeed, thank you. I'd be very honoured to attend, give me half an hour to get ready" replies Malcolm.
"Very good Sir, I'll have a taxi waiting for you."
"Thank you" says Malcolm. The two men leave and Malcolm turns to Leo. "You don't mind to stay behind Leo?"
"Not at all, I have lots more I need to do for tomorrow's run weather permitting." "What would I do without you Leo?"
Leo bends down by the car with a spanner in his hand.

"I'd dread to think, you best get ready, don't want to keep that taxi waiting, you have a nice evening." Malcolm leaves the garage and heads to the hotel to get changed.

HOTEL ROOM

Dorothy can be seen brushing her hair at a dressing table which has perfumes and a make-up bag on it. She is looking into a mirror that is fitted to the dressing table. Malcolm comes in and walks over to the wardrobe and gets out a suit. "Would you like to go out this evening as
I've been invited to a club in town to meet someone?"
Dorothy turns around on the stool she is sitting on.
"Who is it you're meeting" replies Dorothy.
"He's a famous racing driver over here by the name of Frank Lockhart, he's only a young lad but he's won many races."
"Oh I see, well I don't know what to wear."
"You look stunning in what your wearing darling, I must get ready" replies Malcolm.
Malcolm goes into the bathroom to get ready while Dorothy gets out a pair of stockings from the drawer and sits on the bed.
She slides her dress up above her knees and puts her stockings on. She then puts on her shoes and walks back over to the dressing table to apply some make up. Malcolm comes out from the bathroom.
"Here honey, is my tie straight?"
Dorothy gets up and walks over to her husband and goes to straighten his tie. "There you go darling." They both leave the room and head off to the taxi.

DAYTONA CLUB

The club is filled with people sitting at tables that surround
a stage. On the stage is a band playing with a beautiful young woman wearing a short dress and has feathers in her hair who is singing. Her voice drowns out the noise of the people sitting at tables drinking and having a good time.
On one of the tables sits Frank Lockhart and his wife Ella who have guests who are also sitting with him.
Malcolm and his wife enter the club and are met by the Mayor.
"Mr and Mrs Campbell, welcome, I'm very pleased you both could make it, where is your team?"
"They are busy preparing the car for tomorrow."
"Oh what a shame, let me take you over to Mr Lockhart's table" replies the Mayor.

Malcolm and his wife are taking to Frank's table.
"Mr Lockhart, Mr and Mrs Campbell" says the Mayor.
Frank stands up and shakes hands with Malcolm and Dorothy
"It's a pleasure to meet you both, this is my wife Ella."
Ella shakes hands with Dorothy and Malcolm takes Ella's hand and kisses it. "It's great to meet you" says Ella.
They all sit down around the table. "This is one of my mechanics, Chris" says Frank. They shake hands and Malcolm nods his head at him. Ella is sitting opposite Dorothy while Malcolm and Frank start discussing what will be happening the next day. "So Malcolm, it's going to be your first run on an American beach. Do you think you can break the current record?"

Malcolm picks up his glass and leans on the table while Dorothy and Ella are chatting. "Yes, I'd like to think so, I'm certainly going to give it a go and you, I'd love to see your car?" Frank smiles. "Certainly, I'll have her on the beach tomorrow."

"I've read the articles about her that she develops 400hp that's very impressive Frank, I'm just a little bit concerned
that she may be too light for that speed, I take it you're also going to try and break the record" says Malcolm.
"Yes, but I can assure you my dear friend that she'll be quite safe at that speed."
"Let's prey both cars are ok ah!" replies Malcolm.
"I'll drink to that my friend, cheers!"
Malcolm raises his glass to Frank.

The singer is still singing on the stage with the band.
Frank leans across the table to speak to Malcolm
"So tell me Malcolm what size engine do you power your car with?"
"I don't know I just drive the ridden things, it's my mechanic that knows all about the engines."
Malcolm looks across at the pretty singer performing on stage whilst looking sheepish as he doesn't want Frank really knowing the actual details of his car. "Well I wish you all the very best Malcolm."
"Thank you Frank, you too." It's certainly a great club."
They both continue watching the singer on stage while there wife's are chatting to each other.

DAYTONA BEACH FEB 1928.

Daytona Beach is packed with spectators all along the beach with the police keeping the crowd behind a cording.
Malcolm and Frank are posing with their cars for the press.
There wife's are standing close by to the side while the Mayor of Daytona can be seen standing near Malcolm and Frank who are both wearing white overalls.

Malcolm is wearing his brown leather helmet with his goggles around his neck while Frank is wearing a white leather helmet and is wearing his goggles on his head. Both the drivers shake hands with the Mayor. "Good luck to you both, I understand you're not running today Frank" says the Mayor.
"That's correct, I still have some work needs doing to the car and it'll be a couple of days before she'll be ready."
The Mayor walks off while Malcolm looks at Frank's car.
"So hear she is she's quite a looker."

"I wish I could say that for all my girls" says Frank.
"What do you mean, Ella is stunning, you're a very lucky man."
"I know, thank you but she's always moaning."
"Don't they all" replies Malcolm. Frank is looking at Malcolm's car. "I was reading an article in the paper the other day and a Frenchman said your car looked like a whale."

Malcolm laughs. "I heard that too, you wait and see what they say when she beats the record" replies Malcolm. Frank shakes Malcolm's hand. "Well best of luck my friend. Will you be doing the run today?"
"No, I'm just doing a trial run" says Malcolm.
"Ok, good luck" replies Frank. Frank walks away while his team wheel his car away. Malcolm's team are standing around the car and Leo walks up to Malcolm. "How do you feel?"
"If you must know Leo, bloody scared" replies Malcolm.

Malcolm straightens his leather helmet with his hands shaking.
"It's expected I guess it's our first time here but you'll be fine." Leo helps him into the tight cockpit wiping the sand off Malcolm's shoes before he climbs right in.

The team stands ready waiting for the all clear to proceed from the officials to do a trial run with Malcolm nervously waiting in the car. Leo is standing next to Malcolm who's sitting in the car. Malcolm looks up.
"Tyres good Leo?" Leo looks over to Steve Macdonald from the Dunlop Company whose looking after the tyres.
"How are the tyres looking Steve?"
"There all good Leo."
"Great, Joe are we all set?"
Joe from Napier looks across to his partner also from Napier.
"Everything all tuned and ready to go Walter" says Joe.
"All checked Joe" says Leo. Joe looks back at Leo with thumbs up. "All ready to go Leo" says Joe.
"Great, let's do this, standby to start her up Joe."
Joe wheels the gas starter and plugs it into start the
Bluebird's 800hp aero engine.

Smoke pours out of the exhausts as the engine roars into life
and the team start to push the car forward along the beach to
straighten her up for her test run.
They all wait anxiously for the officials to give the all clear to go. Malcolm is nervously gripping the steering wheel.
He selects first gear and waits. The officials give the signal to go. Malcolm gets underway as he accelerates from his team heading south along the beach.

Malcolm fights to control the car as its slipping and sliding
on the hard sand. He gets the car up to 100mph when he hits an uneven bit of sand and sends the Bluebird up into the air and back down hitting the sand very hard which brings out the back end of the car and a piece of the under-shield flies off and is thrown into the air as the car speeds along. Malcolm has to fight to correct the skid and he gets the car under control.
Malcolm finally slows the car down and comes to a stop and switches the engine off.

Malcolm leans back in his seat, he is injured.
His seat is damaged by the impact and he has hurt his back.
Malcolm's team can be seen running towards him and an ambulance is racing towards Malcolm.
Malcolm slowly manages to pull himself out of the car.
As he walks away he looks back at the car. The team reach him and can see Malcolm is limping badly.
Leo puts Malcolm's arm around his waist while Joe and Walter check the Bluebird over.
"Jesus Christ! The suspension mounts are damaged."
Joe is looking at the underside of the car.
"Where the heck has that gone!"
Joe looks back at where the car has come from and sees a
policeman carrying a curled up piece of metal.
"I think this is yours, we saw it fly off the machine."
Joe takes it off the policeman. "Thanks."
The policeman looks across at Malcolm.
"Is he going to be alright?" says the policeman.

"I sure hope so" says Joe. The team sort the car out as a tow truck appears on the beach and Leo helps Malcolm head back to the hotel.

DAYTONA BEACH 19TH FEBUARY 1928

Several days later the team are back and have fixed the car with Malcolm fully recovered. Frank Lockhart is in the distance with his car the Black Hawk. Malcolm and Frank greet each other. "Don't mind if I go first Frank?"
"Sure thing Malcolm, you go ahead good luck." They both part and head to their cars. Malcolm gets in his car with his team standing around it waiting for the all clear from the officials. One of the officials gives the all clear to go for the attempt and the engine roars into life. Malcolm's team can be seen running behind the Bluebird as it speeds off down the beach.
Malcolm accelerates sand flying up and around the car.
The crowd are seen cheering as the Bluebird roars past.
Malcolm flies through the measured mile at about 208mph and slows the car down to turn it around for the second run.
As he slows down he loses the back end again but manages to control it and lines the car up for his second and final run.
He flies through the measured mile just over 207mph.
Malcolm slows the car down and drives up to his team that are rushing towards him. He stops the car and turns the engine off while Leo rushes up to Malcolm. "I think you've done it boss! That looked very fast" says Leo. Malcolm takes his goggles off and hands them to Leo.
Malcolm's hands are still shaking as he takes his leather helmet off and hands it to Leo as the rest of the team frantically undo panels on the car so it can cool down.
Steam can be seen coming from the radiators.
Malcolm is helped out of the car by Leo.

In the distance are the timing officials followed by Frank Lockhart and his team anxious to find out if Malcolm has broken the record. Malcolm brushes himself down and is approached by the officials.
"A great result Captain Campbell, a new world record of 206.956mph, congratulations Sir!" says the official.

The official hands Malcolm the slip of paper with the timings and speed on it. The crowd are cheering. Frank is looking back along the beach where the
Bluebird had just made its run, clutching his white leather helmet and looking eager he walks back to his car with his team standing around it. Franks team are preparing the Stutz Black Hawk for its trial run. One of his team members is polishing the white body work of the car while another is checking the tyres. Frank stands next to the car while the team are busy. Ella runs up to Frank and gives him a hug and a kiss. "Good luck honey!" she says. "Thanks dear."

<u>Frank Lockhart standing next to his Stutz Black Hawk at Daytona.</u>

Ella walks away and Frank puts on his white leather helmet and is approached by one of the officials.
"Mr Lockhart, I understand that this is going to be a trial run?"
"Yes, indeed it is Sir, Could you record my speed?"
"Of course, we can do that for you; give us the signal when you're ready to do the run" says the official.
"Ok, thank you" says Frank.
Frank turns back to his team while the official heads back to the timing stands. Frank is passed his gloves by his crew.
"Cars ready and set for the run Frank, do you need anything?"
"No, I think I'm fine, let's do this!" replies Frank.
Frank places one hand on the body of the car and looks at the car up and down whilst holding his gloves in the other.

The team help Frank into the car. Frank puts on his gloves.
One of the officials can be seen giving the thumbs up to the team that there ready. The police can be seen keeping the spectators behind the cordon as Franks team push the car forward to line it up along the beach. "Ok Frank start her up!" says one of the team members.

Frank fires the Black Hawk up. The car roars into life. Frank puts it into 1st gear and the team push him away.
Frank moves up the gears and reaches 181mph and slows the car down to turn round and head back up the beach back to his team. The crowd are cheering. Frank drives the car back to his team and stops the car. He turns the engine off and is helped out of the car. Malcolm and Leo are walking up to Frank.
"Well done Frank, that looked fast, how do you feel kid?"
Frank takes his gloves off and wipes his face.
"I feel that went well, I feel she can go faster, much faster!"
"Just make sure you weight the car down cos as you hit 200mph you'll take off if you hit a bump," says Malcolm.
"I'm sure I'll be fine Malcolm, Thanks for the advice."

Frank Lockhart sitting in his Black Hawk on Daytona Beach Florida.

Malcolm and Leo look around the Black Hawk while Frank takes off his leather helmet. Malcolm and Leo walk back to their team who are standing around the Bluebird.
"Frank must be crazy if he thinks he can push that car over 200mph and still keep it on the ground, it's too light!"
"Let him find out for himself. What do you want to do about the Bluebird? You still think she can do better" says Leo.
"Yes I do we'll bring her back here in the next couple of days. They walk off together while Frank and his team start moving the Black Hawk off the beach.

DAYTONA BEACH 22ND FEB 1928

Both contenders to the land speed record attempt are back on the beach with their teams and their cars. Malcolm is seen examining the beach, Frank and his team looking on in the background. Leo walks up to Malcolm.
"What do you think? Is it smooth enough" says Leo.
"No, look at it Leo, it's got more bumps in it than a French street circuit this time Frank can go first." Malcolm walks towards his Bluebird. Frank walks up to Malcolm and his team.
"Hello chaps, what a glorious morning it is" says Frank.
"It certainly is kid, you going to go first?"
"I'd be delighted Mr Campbell, Thank you."

Frank heads for his team who are waiting by the car while
Malcolm and his team watch. "Should we be worried Leo?"
"I'm not sure; I still think your right, it's too light for the speed" says Leo. Frank is getting ready for the attempt with thousands of spectators looking on from his left as Frank's team make final preparations to the Black Hawk car.
Ella rushes up to Frank and gives him a hug. "Now you take care darling and good luck." Frank smiles at Ella as she helps him to do up his leather helmet. She kisses him on the cheek and walks off. Frank is helped into the car by the team while Malcolm and his team look on.

Frank is giving the go ahead signal from the timing officials and he starts the 16 cylinder engine. It roars into life with smoke coming out of the side exhausts. With the crowd cheering Frank selects 1st gear and he's underway with a push from his team as they run alongside him until they can't keep up. Heading north along the beach Frank puts the car into 2nd and picks up speed going ever faster ducking his head behind his little glass windshield.
Now doing over 120mph he puts it up into third with the sound of the engine roaring as it passes the rows of watching spectators who are cheering. Frank changes up into top gear and put his foot hard down on the accelerator pedal and is now doing well over 150mph with sand flicking up around the car.
He is gripping the steering wheel hard when suddenly the car goes over an uneven patch of sand which lifts the car up in the air and back down on the hard sand and makes the back end of the car spin out of control.

As the car spins around sideways the wheels dig into the sand and flick the car into the air several times before crashing into the sea. Frank is still sitting in the car with the sea lapping the sides of the car as spectators rush towards the wrecked car and try to pull Frank out of the car but he appears to be stuck. At the other end of the beach Malcolm and the others are looking on not knowing what has happened.
"I'm sure I heard the engine cut out."
"You sure" says Leo.
"Yes, I think something's wrong."
A man runs towards Malcolm and the team.
"He's crashed! It doesn't look good."
Malcolm's team are shocked.
"I told him that car is too light for that speed, now look what's happened." Malcolm turns to the man.
"How bad is he?"
"I'm not sure; I think he's still stuck in the car."
The man runs back up the beach towards the accident.
In the distance the sound of an ambulance can be heard.

The spectators manage to pull Frank free from the wreckage and
drag him a couple of meters away from the car. They lay his body down on the beach while the police supervise. Frank is still alive but he has broken ribs and his leg is broken. Ella is fighting through the

crowd to get to Frank who is lying on the beach helpless. She grabs hold of one of his arms with tears running down her face and kneeling next to him. "Baby talk to me" weeps Ella.
Frank runs his hand through her hair. "Those dam bumps darling." Frank lays his head back down on the sand as the ambulance crews arrive to put him in the ambulance and take him to hospital. Ella climbs into the ambulance and it speeds off while a tow truck arrives to pull the wrecked Black Hawk out of the sea.

DAYTONA HOSPITAL

A couple of days later Frank is laying in hospital with his
wife by his bedside. The doctor walks in.
"Hi Mr Lockhart, how are you feeling" says the Doctor.
"A lot better but still sore, thanks for all you've done for me" replies Frank. "You're very welcome. Are you feeling up for a visit from someone special?"
"Yes doctor, who is it?"
"It's Captain Campbell and his wife, shall I send them both in? "Yes of course, thank you Doctor."
Malcolm and his wife enter the room. "How you feeling kid, that was quiet a scare you gave us."
"Yes it was" replies Frank. Ella holds Franks hand.
"I've think he's very brave" says Ella.
"Yes indeed you are kid and I wish you a speedy recovery."
"I hear your rebuilding the car, when do you reckon it'll be finished" says Malcolm.
"Next couple of months I hope."
"Well it's great to see you getting better, you take care Frank" says Malcolm. Malcolm and his wife leave.

ROBIN HOOD ENGINEERING
LONDON

Mechanics are working on a very long chassis. One man is tightening up a nut with a spanner. The vehicle being built is the Golden Arrow and it is resting on wooden beams raised a few inches off the factory floor with a mechanic working underneath it.
An engine is fitted to the chassis partly covered by a gold coloured cowling moulded to the shape of the engine block.
There are no wheels fitted to the chassis and only has a few
body panels fitted to it which is also painted gold.
At the front of the chassis it has a gold chiselled nose and at the rear of the chassis no panels have yet been fitted so you can see the framework of what appears to be the shape of a tail fin.
There are two men dressed in suits and ties and one of them is
wearing a hat who are standing to the side of the front of the
chassis watching the mechanics working. Their names are Louis Coatalen and Jack Irving and are watching with excitement.

POVEY CROSS 1928

Malcolm and Leo are sitting around the dinner table looking at
a map of Africa. The dog is lying nearby. Dorothy can be heard in the kitchen preparing food.
Malcolm looks at the map with a pipe in his mouth. "This is where I'd like to make our next attempt Leo, right here" says Malcolm.
Malcolm points to the map with Leo looking on.
"What's the area called? I can't quiet read it" says Leo.

"It's called Verneuk Pan and it's a dried up lake 450 miles from Cape Town."
"Ok" replies Leo. Dorothy brings in some food and places it on the table. "I'm going out there very soon to survey the area and whilst I'm out there I'd like you to continue supervising the production of the new car while I'm away" says Malcolm.
"Sure thing boss." They both continue looking at the map as Dorothy brings in more food to put on the table.

ROBIN HOOD ENGINEERING
LONDON

Men can be seen still working on the Golden Arrow car with
Henry and Louis watching on. The car now has wheels and the tail panels have now been fitted. Louis, Jack and Henry are looking on. "It's coming along nicely Jack, how soon you think she'll be ready?" says Henry. "Hopefully in the next couple of months, there's still an awful lot to do" replies Jack.
The men watch on as the engineers work on her.

DAYTONA BEACH 22ND APRIL 1928

Crowds of people are lined up along one side of a beach
facing the sea. A tall stocky man wearing white overalls and a white racing cap can be seen standing next to a large black car with four wheels. The man's name is Ray Keech and the car is called the White Triplex 'Spirit of Elkdom and he has just broken the land speed record at a speed of 207.55 mph beating Malcolm's record. He is talking to the press.

Ray Keech

DAYTONA BEACH 25TH APRIL 1928

Thousands of spectators line the beach held back by a long
cordon that stretches along the beach. At the northern far end of the beach is Frank Lockhart, his wife and his team and there all standing around the Black Hawk car posing for the press who are taking photograph's. An official walks up to Frank. "Timing instruments are all ready to go Mr Lockhart."

"Thank you kind Sir" replies Frank. The press move away from the car as the team get it ready for the run. Ella has her arms around Frank's waist as Frank watches over his team getting the car ready. "Be careful dear" says Ella. Frank smiles. "You know I will" replies Frank smiling.

Frank kisses his wife and Ella walks off to the side where all
the spectators are standing. Frank puts on his gloves and approaches the side of the car. One of the officials walks over to Frank. "The beach is in a terrible mess due to the recent activities Sir, It might be worth waiting for the following season, what do you want to do Sir?"
"I'll make the attempt if that's ok" replies Frank.
One of Frank's mechanics walks up behind Frank and places his
hand on his arm. "He's got a point Frank; look at the state of the beach "It'll be fine, let's start her up" says Frank.
Frank is helped into the car and the team prepare to start her
up. Ella looks on whilst standing amongst the crowd.
Frank is smiling and waving to his wife from the
cockpit of the Black Hawk as the team gives the thumbs up to
Frank to start her up. Ella is smiling back whilst holding both hands together up to her mouth.

The sound of the 16 cylinder engine can be heard as it roars
into live. The spectators cheer and the team push the Black Hawk away on its record attempt. Frank drives the Black Hawk north and slowly turns it around to drive south down the beach. He picks up speed and the crowd cheer. Frank selects a higher gear and the car picks up speed. Faster and faster he goes with sand and dust trailing behind. The Black Hawk is now doing 220mph.

A plane is flying in the sky filming Frank's record attempt.
Frank starts to slow the Black Hawk down so he can turn around
and do the second run. He accidently locks up the rear brakes and the tyres scrape along the hard sand. He managers to control the car and comes to a stop and gets out of the car.
He makes a quick inspection of the tyres and climbs back into
the car and heads back up the beach heading north. The crowd are cheering him on as Ella looks on. Frank picks up speed and is going at about 225mph when suddenly one of his rear tyres explodes ripping all the cowling off that's surrounding the wheel.

The Black Hawk swerves to the right and then to the left and
starts to slide side wards along the beach. As its sliding side wards it hits an uneven piece of sand that courses the Black Hawk to flip into the air several times until it lands back on the beach throwing Frank out of the cockpit and hard onto the beach.
The Black Hawk rests near where Frank's body lies.
The crowd are in shock at what they've just witnessed.
Ella is standing amongst them screaming.
Some members of the crowd rush over to where Frank's body lies
whilst police and team members put out the smouldering Black Hawk. An ambulance's bell can be heard in the distance as Frank's lifeless body is covered with a blanket.
One of the spectators who is helping cover the body looks over
towards Ella and shakes his head to let her know that her husband is dead. Ella falls to her knees crying as spectators standing around her try to comfort her. The ambulance arrives on the scene. The ambulance doors open and stretcher bearers get out and move towards the incident.

The remains of the Stutz Black Hawk that killed Frank Lockhart 1928.

SUNBEAM FACTORY WOLVERHAMPTON

Henry is standing at a desk looking at drawings with Louis.
Jack comes into the office and hands Henry a newspaper.
"Sorry for the interruption but you need to read this."
Henry starts reading the paper. Louis looks on with interest.
"Well what is it" replies Louis.
"It's that young lad from America; He's only gone and killed himself whilst attempting to break the land speed record at Daytona" says Henry. They all appear to be surprised and shocked as Henry continues. "It says hear that he achieved an average speed of 220mph before the incident."
Jack comes closer to Henry who hands the paper to Louis.

"That's not the only bad thing that happened; his wife saw everything and was only feet away from where he landed."
Louis and Henry suddenly look shocked. "Jesus Christ, that's terrible! Poor woman having to witness that" says Henry.
"Did you know that he had just turned 26 years of age, poor sod" says Louis. "What actually happened" says Henry.
"Says his tyre blew at speed and made the car flip over several times throwing him out of the cockpit" replies Louis.
Henry shakes his head. "It seems this pursuit for speed is getting increasingly dangerous" says Henry.
"You're certainly right Henry that's why we must make these cars saver" replies Jack.
"Good to hear it, right best be off, see you all later chaps".
"Yes Henry, see you very soon" says Jack.
"Ok great" says Henry.

MR WHITE'S GARAGE FLORIDA

Ray Keech is standing in front of a desk with a man dressed in a suit standing behind it. They are leaning over the desk looking at plans of a racing car known as the White Triplex which is the current land speed record holder.
The man standing behind the desk is Mr White and is the designer of the White Triplex. In the corner of the room is another man in a suit who is helping with the finance and development of the car. "Well Ray, we have given her more horse power and tightened up on the suspension, should be enough to keep the record in the hands of the US for a while" says Mr White. "I hear that Henry Segrave is coming back to Daytona with a new car" replies Ray. "I heard that too, they call it the Golden Arrow and it's supposed to do a speed of about 220mph" says Mr White. "220mph! You sure the Triplex is going to beat that" replies Ray. "Of course it will, don't worry" says Ray.
The man in the suit standing behind Ray moves towards him and places his hand on Ray's shoulder. "We've made all the necessary modifications to beat Segrave's new car. You don't have to worry about the control of it at that speed because it'll be fine". Ray looks baffled. "What do you mean? If you think I'm driving that again, you're very much mistaken, you need to find another driver" says Ray.
"Come on Ray, I thought you wanted to do this" says Mr White. "No way, there are loads of other racing drivers that will gladly take my seat, I'm out". Ray turns to leave the office. "Who do you suggest Ray" replies Mr White. Ray turns round. "I don't know at the top of my head".
"How about asking Lee if he wants to drive the car" says the man in the suit. "No way, he's a mechanic" snaps Ray.
"No harm in asking him I suppose".
"You've inserted the Grim Reaper into those engines and he's just waiting to come out" replies Ray.
Ray goes to the office door and turns around.
"I'm sorry Mr White but I won't be driving her this time".
Ray leaves the office. "See what Lee Bible says, if he doesn't want to take Ray's place then will have to look elsewhere" says Mr White. "Ok will do Mr White" replies the man in the suit. The man leaves the office.

DAYTONA BEACH 25TH FEBRUARY 1929

Thousands of people are surrounding a gold coloured car with a few men dressed in white overalls standing around it.
The car is called the Golden Arrow and the team are here to do a test run of the car. The car belongs to Jack Irving and will be driven by Henry Segrave who is also standing by the car.
The police are standing by the team forming a cordon as Jack and Henry explain to the press about the test run.

"The Golden Arrow has a W12 Napier Lion engine powering her which develops 925hp and we hope that she will be capable of
240mph we hope" says Henry.
Henry laughs as do the press that have gathered around the team. "When do you think you shall be ready for the actual attempt." asks the reporter. Henry looks at Jack. "Hopefully in the next couple of days. Ok thank you" says Jack.

The Golden Arrow before its test run on Daytona Beach.

The police start clearing space for the test run.
Henry puts his white helmet on as Doris walks up to him.
"Take care darling," says Doris. She kisses him on the cheek.
"Not to worry dear, this is just going to be a test run, it shouldn't take long," replies Henry. "Ok darling, be safe."
Doris walks off to the side while Jack walks up to the car and speaks to the team. "Right then chaps, I want things checked and double checked. I don't want any mistakes," says Jack.
Henry walks up to the team while putting his gloves on.
"All set to go lads?"
"All set Henry; we've tightened up the suspension and lowered your clutch pedal as you've asked," replies the team member.
"Cheers lads." They help Henry climb into the car and Henry is seen checking his instruments. One of the team members carries round the gas starter to start the engine and places it to the side of the car.
Jack walks to the side of the Golden Arrow and checks the sighting scope in front of the windshield is firmly fitted. Henry looks over the windshield at Jack. "Do you think I'll need that?"
"I can hardly see past it let alone through it," says Henry.

"It's to help you line up the car."
"We can take it off later if it's a hindrance. In the mean time I'd like you to try it," replies Jack.

"Ok, I'll give it a go." The team prepare to start the car and are waiting for the thumbs up from Henry while Jack steps back. The team check the gas starter is securely connected. The team all look at Henry. "Ok, set, start her up," says Henry.
The team crank the gas starter and smoke is seen coming from the exhausts as the engine roars into life. The team push the car away and Henry speeds off along the beach in a southerly direction. Henry is fighting to keep her straight as he gets up to speed with sand spraying up around the car. Henry slows the car down to turn around and head back the other way. He picks up speed again and roars past all the spectators who are all cheering including Henry's wife Doris. Henry hits 180mph and gradually tries to slow the car down. He drives the Golden Arrow up to his team. Jack runs up to the side of the car.
"Well how was it," says Jack.
Henry looks exhausted trying to catch a breath. "Bloody terrible."
"Is it the engine, gearbox," replies Jack.
"It's neither, I can't bloody see anything."
"There must be too much glare coming off the body work," says one of Henry's team mates looking at the body work shining in the sun. "What do you suggest we do about it Jack," says Henry. "We could always paint the areas black that are causing the problem," replies Jack.
"Then that would mean painting everything forward from where I'm sitting black, you alright with that Jack?"
Jack scratches his head as Doris walks up to the side of the car. "I suppose I'll have to be Henry, it's your safety I'm concerned about and getting the record."
"That's not just the only thing, I'm having problems with the gun sight, I just can't see though it at speed and it needs to come off Jack."
"Ok, let's pack her up and start doing the modifications."

The team start getting ready to tow the car back to the garage as Henry climbs out of the car. He kisses his wife.
"Told you I wouldn't be long." Henry then walks up to Jack who's examining the car. "You've built an incredible machine Jack and should be proud of her." Jack places his hands on his waist. "I am and I'll be even more when she breaks the record." Henry takes off his helmet.
"Is there any way of getting another helmet as this one nearly took my head off as I looked over the windshield, I think it's this bit on the helmet that is a wind trap, I'll need one that doesn't have one," says Henry.
Jack looks at the helmet. "I've seen some helmets without this in motorcycle racing I'll get one for you," replies Jack.
Henry looks around then looks back at Jack.
"I think it's going to take more than a couple of days to get the car ready, don't you think Jack?"
"Yes, I think your right Henry, I'll inform the press."
Jack heads off to inform the press as Henry watches the team preparing the car to be towed off the beach.

DAYTONA BEACH 11TH MARCH 1929

About 120'000 spectators line the beach.
At the far end of the beach by the pier can be seen more lines of people and are all looking to there right hand side.
A sudden loud noise of an engine can be heard near them.

Out from amongst the lines of people appears the Golden Arrow car driven by Henry Segrave. There is a police motorcycle riding alongside Henry. The Golden Arrow is completely Black in colour with Black spoked wheels.

The Golden Arrow painted Black before the record attempt 1929.

Henry drives up to a group of photographers that have gathered up ahead and turns off the engine. Henry's team rush towards him as he gets out of the car.
Henry climbs out and walks over to the photographers and is greeted by his wife Doris. They are both joined by Jack Irving. The press are kneeling in front of them holding pencils and notepads. "What speed will you be hoping to achieve today Mr Segrave?" asks one of the reporters.
"I'm not sure, you'll have to just wait and see," says Henry.
The police move the press away so they can get the car ready for its run. Henry is wearing his white overalls and his white helmet and prepares to climb into the car.
Henry's team are working on the car getting her ready as one of his team members puts Black discs onto the wheels and is seen tightening them up. Another team member is carrying a small gas generator by its handle and places it by the side of the Golden Arrow car.
The gas generator has hoses coming out of it and they are inserted into the engine compartment of the Golden Arrow.
Doris walks other to Henry who is sitting in the Golden Arrow and kisses him on the cheek. "Good luck dear."
Henry smiles at her. "Thank you. See you in a short while dear." Jack walks over to Henry as Doris goes off to stand with the crowd that are watching. "How do you feel, all set to go?" says Jack. Henry looks at his instruments on the dashboard. "Yes I think so."
"Ok Henry, best of luck," replies Jack.
Jack goes off to stand with Doris as the team prepare to start the Golden Arrow car. "Set to go Henry?"
"Ok turn her over," replies Henry.
The 925hp Napier engine roars into live and the team push Henry away heading south. Henry gets the car into a higher gear and slowly picks up speed as sand starts flicking up around it. Henry flies through the measured mile at about 230mph. A plane flies overhead filming the run.
Henry slows the car down as he approaches his team.

The team get the car ready for the return run.
"Come on, we need to hurry up or the engines going to overheat," yells Henry. The team hurry and turn the car around and set Henry on his return run. Picking up speed he tries to keep the car straight. Faster and faster he goes as he flies back through the measured mile.

Passing the measured mile on Daytona Beach.

He slows the car down and drives towards his team who are waiting for him while the crowd are cheering. Henry pulls up to his team and turns the engine off.

Jack runs up to the side of the car. "I think you've done it Henry!" Doris can be seen leaning over a fence waving at her husband Henry.
Henry waves back at her. A timing official runs up to Henry and the team carrying a piece of paper.

"Well done Sir a new world record!" says the official.
Jack takes the piece of paper and reads it. He jumps up and down with excitement. "A speed of 231mph Henry. Well done."
Henry smiles as he is lifted onto the shoulders of his team and is carried off in the distance with photographers following behind trying to get a picture.

HOTEL CAPE TOWN AFRICA

Malcolm, Dorothy, Leo and the rest of the team are sitting
round a dinner table eating when a waiter comes into the room
and hands Malcolm a bit of paper. Malcolm reads it and shrugs his shoulders. "What is it dear?" says Dorothy. "It's about Henry Segrave; he's gone and smashed the record in that car built by Jack Irving" replies Malcolm.
Leo looks over to Dorothy and then looks at Malcolm.
"What was the speed?" says Leo. "231mph. Not bad a Leo?"

"If you say so boss, where does that leave us with the Bluebird?" I don't know, but I'm not going to pack up and go home, I'm determined to give it a go first. "Ok" says Leo.
Leo looks over to Dorothy and they continue to eat.

DAYTONA BEACH 13TH MARCH 1929

Crowds of spectators line the beach. Two cars are lined up next to each other.
The two cars are the Golden Arrow and the White Triplex.
Standing next to them are Henry Segrave and Lee Bible who is accompanied by the Triplex designer Mr J M White who are all posing for the press. "Are you ready to take back the record for the United States Mr Bible?" says one of the reporters.
"Indeed I am" replies Lee Bible
Lee shakes hands with Henry Segrave and goes off towards his team while Henry goes off to speak with his team.
"Is she ready to take it back off him if he succeeds in breaking the record?" asks Henry.
"Yes Henry, she's all been tuned up to give us that little bit more horse power" replies the team mechanic.
Good. Henry and the team watch as Lee and his team prepare the Triplex for the run.

They start the Triplex up and its three engines roar into live. Lee Bible selects first gear and he's away heading south along the beach.
He flies past the timing tower at high speed.
He struggles to slow the car down and manages to turn the car around and head back up the beach. As he's doing about 120mph something goes wrong and the car spins out of control.
Further up the beach is a cameraman standing filming the event. His name is Charles Traub of Pathe News Company.
Charles sees the Triplex coming towards him and runs out of the way only to be hit by the out of control Triplex and his camera remained still standing on the tripod.
The Triplex continued to roll until it came to rest up against a sand dune throwing Lee out of the cockpit and land at the feet of his wife.
The crowd all look shocked. People run over to the wreckage while some go over to see to the bodies of Lee and the cameraman, Charles. They can be seen to confirm that they've both been killed as they bow their heads whilst standing around the bodies.
At the wreckage of the Triplex a man can be seen pulling one of Lee Bible's shoes that were still inside the mangled cockpit. Henry Segrave can be seen looking at the wreckage.
He turns around to Jack who's standing next to him.
"Once we have raced against Gar Wood we are going home" he says. "What about the Golden Arrow, she'll easily increase the record?" replies Jack. "No, that's the last time I drive her and that's final."
Henry turns and walks away while Jack continues to look at the men sifting through the wreckage.

Lee Bible.

HOTEL ROOM FLORIDA

Henry is sitting at a dressing table being comforted by his wife Doris after the tragic incident of Lee Bible.

Louis Coatalen walks in the room. "The cars been packed up Henry and is ready to be shipped back to England, you still want to do this race against Gar Wood? Henry looks up and runs his hands along his scalp. "Of course Louis."
"Ok, that's great."
"Is the boat all ready?"
"Yes, she's good to go, by the way we've been invited to a club and I think you both need to go."
"Ok I could do with a drink" replies Henry.
Henry goes on to race Gar Wood and wins and when Henry returned back to England he was knighted.

MALCOLMS WORKSHOP BROOKLANDS

Several weeks have passed and Malcolm and his team are preparing to disassemble the old Bluebird that's sitting outside the workshop with a sheet over it. Inside the workshop is a man dressed in a suit wearing glasses and his name is Reid Railton. He is talking to the team whilst holding a set of plans for the new Bluebird car. Malcolm is outside smoking a pipe whilst looking at the old Bluebird which is still covered by a sheet. Dorothy appears driving Malcolm's Mercedes racing car.
She turns off the ignition and gets out of the car and walks up to her husband. "This car has cost me a lot of money dear and I just hope our next project is less costly." says Malcolm. Dorothy holds on to Malcolm's arm.
"I'm sure it's going to be fine this time just promise me we're not going back to Africa. That venture was bad luck from the start." says Dorothy. "I promise I feel things are finally on the up." He kisses his wife on the cheek and they both head into the garage. Inside the garage the team are looking over the plans for the new Bluebird with their new designer Reid Railton.

SUNBEAM FACTORY WOLVERHAMPTON JAN 1930

Men in white overalls can be seen working on a long frame structure that is raised off the floor.
In one corner of the factory are two engines that are being worked on by two men also dressed in white overalls.
One man is standing in front of them wearing a hat and an overcoat with his hands in his coat pockets. The man is Louis Coatalen and is watching his mechanics building a new car for the land speed record attempt.

Sir Henry Segrave walks in. Louis turns round to greet him.
"Well here he is. Am I to call you Sir now my old friend?"
Henry laughs and goes to shake Louis's hand.
"Of course not, it's me that should be calling you Sir as I owe you for where I am today." Louis waves his hands at Henry and turns his head. "Ah, you're too modest old chum."
"So what you working on, I hear from Jack that you're developing a new land speed record machine?" says Henry.
They both walk towards the mechanics who are working on the new machine. "This is our new project and were going to name her, the Silver Bullet; we hope to get her up to 300mph."
Henry looks surprised." I hope you're not going to ask me to drive it." Louis laughs. "Of course not we have a driver in mind; his name is Kaye Don the Irish racing driver."

"When do you hope to be ready Louis?"
"Sometime in the next couple of months, the teams working round the clock to get her ready."
"Well good luck with that" says Henry.
"Yes I think we're going to need it, you see Henry were running out of money, its expensive business this record breaking lark.

"So you reckon this is going to be your last one?"
"I'm afraid so Henry. "Anyway how's your water speed attempt coming along?"
"Yeah it's going great; we should be ready to go in the summer."
"Well I wish you all the best with that Henry."
They both shake hands. "Thank you. Henry leaves the factory.

DAYTONA BEACH MARCH 1930

The Sunbeam team are on the beach with Kaye Don and Louis
Coatalen with the Silver Bullet car. They pose for the press then get the car ready for its run. They connect a gas starter to start the two 2.000hp aero engines.
"All ready to go Sir?" says a team member.
"Yes start her up." replies Kaye.
The car roars into live as black smoke pours out of the exhaust. Kaye Don puts the car into first gear and he's off heading south down the beach slowly picking up speed as sand is flicked up around the car by the tyres.
He flies through the measured mile at about 180mph and slowly slows the huge car down to turn it around and go back the other way. The crowd cheer as Kaye gets back up to speed and roars past them at over 100mph heading north up the beach.
He flies through the measured mile at about 187mph. He slows the car down and heads for his team who are waiting up ahead. Kaye pulls up to his team and leans out of the car.
"It's no good she won't go any faster." With the engines still running the team start undoing some of the cars body panels to see why she isn't doing the full speed she should be doing. As one of the team members looks into the engine he can see oil dripping from the bottom of the car. "Quick! Get a rag she's dripping oil." As the team member is giving a rag the bottom of the car suddenly catches fire and the team members rush about trying to put the fire out. Kaye can see the fire coming out of the car and jumps out. "Jesus come on hurry up and put it out" yells Kaye. "We can't run her again when this has happened; we're going to have to take her back for repairs." Alright" replies Kaye. The team member beckons the truck to come over. The team put out the fire and the truck pulls up to tow the Silver Bullet car away.

The Silver Bullet at its factory.

BROOKLANDS 1930

Dorothy is standing next to Leo with her arms crossed as mechanics are working on the new Bluebird car. "The car is coming along splendidly Leo."
"It most certainly is Dorothy, I'm very pleased with our progress, it won't be long before we ship her out to Daytona."
Dorothy starts to walk around the car while Leo checks the work with one of the mechanics. "Make sure these struts are strong; I don't want them coming loose and touching the wheels" says Leo. "Will do boss" replies the mechanic.
"Leo, what's this in aid of?" asks Dorothy.
Dorothy is pointing to a streamlined metal object on top of the engine cowling. Leo walks over and explains to her.
"It's a rev counter so Malcolm can continue looking straight ahead and not down at his instruments."
"Oh I see." A very good idea Leo." They both continue inspecting the car.

LAKE WINDERMERE 13TH JUNE 1930

Several people can be seen standing on the banks of a lake watching Sir Henry Segrave putting on his white leather cap and is joined by his chief mechanic Victor Helliwell and another mechanic called Michael Willcocks.
They are preparing to set a new water speed record in a long speed boat called Miss England 2 that can be seen moored up against the dock.
The boat is white with Miss England written on the side of it and is powered by two Rolls-Royce Schneider engines.
Both engines give out 4500hp and have two large exhausts sticking out of them facing forward just behind the three seats that are all next to each other.

Henry Segrave.

The men prepare to climb into the boat and Henry is seen waving to his wife Doris as he climbs in. Men who are standing on the landing station detaches the rope and throws it to Victor who is seated next to Henry.
Victor pushes the boat away from the side with the help of the men standing on the landing station.
As there pushed away Henry's mechanic Michael sitting on his right side can be seen trying to start the engines with the help of Henry.
There a sudden popping sound and black smoke appearing around the engines when a mighty roar is heard as the engines come to life. The crowd on the side of the lake start cheering.
Henry pushes the throttle forward and the boat speeds off into the distance. Faster and faster they go as they speed through the measured mile at about 96mph.
Henry slows the boat down just enough so he can turn her around and head back the other way.
The boat picks up speed as it goes past the crowd who are cheering. Henry takes the boat through the measured mile.

This time, going at 100mph he slows the boat down and looks over to his chief mechanic. "Well I think we've done it old chap, I think she'll go faster, how about another pass Victor?" shouts Henry. "I think your right, let's go."
On the side of the lake Doris is looking on with excitement as one of the timing officials approaches her.
"They've done it my lady congratulations your husband now holds the water speed record as well as the land speed record."
"That's great news; he will be pleased thank you."

One of the spectators points out towards the far end of the lake. "Do they know they've broken the record cos it looks like there going again" says the man. Doris looks up to where the man is pointing

and sees the speed boat screaming towards them in the distance. All of a sudden it appears that the boat hits something in the water which causes the boat to somersault and capsize landing on top of Victor and throws Michael clear of the boat and into the water breaking his arm.
As for Henry he is seen floating on the water unconscious.
Doris starts screaming frantically as she almost falls into the lake only to be held back by the crowd. Other boats start rushing to the scene. They help lift the bodies out of the water and head back to the landing stations to where there is an ambulance waiting with stretchers. In the distance is the up turned hull of the boat Miss England as the ambulance takes Henry and Victor to the nearby hotel while Michael is seen wearing a blanket over him getting into a car.

HOTEL ROOM

Doris sitting at Henry's bedside holding his lifeless hand as a doctor can be seen checking his pulse. "I'm very sorry my dear but his injuries are to great and there be very little I can do." Doris sobs. Suddenly Henry squeezes Doris's hand and opens his eyes and looks up at her as the doctor leans towards him. "Henry, can you hear me?" says Doris. "How are Michael and Victor?" says Henry in a quiet voice. Doris shakes her head. "Victor was killed but Michael's going to be ok."

The doctor places his stethoscope on Henry's chest. "I love you." says Doris squeezing his hand. "I love you too. Did I break the record?"
"Yes, 98.76mph" Henry gasps for air and slowly passes away.
"Henry!" says Doris squeezing his hand tighter as the doctor takes his stethoscope from out of his ears. "I'm very sorry my dear but he's gone." Doris sobs and kisses Henry's hand.

POVEY CROSS

Dorothy is outside the garage putting oil into a car.
She is wearing white overalls and has her sleeves rolled up and is servicing one of Malcolm's racing cars, a 750hp Austin.
A postman riding a bicycle pulls up and rests his bicycle up against the fence and walks up to Dorothy and hands her a telegram from his bag.
The postman leaves and Dorothy places the telegram on the side of the racing car whilst she wipes her hands with an old rag.
Then she opens the telegram and starts reading it.
The look of shock appears on her face as she places one hand over her mouth.
She folds the telegram up and places it in her pocket and starts closing the engine compartment of the racing car and runs towards the garage and closes the garage doors.
Then she jumps into the Austin racing car, starts her up and drives off out of Povey Cross towards Brooklands.

BROOKLANDS

Leo is outside one of Malcolm's garages where there working on the new Napier Railton Bluebird. Leo is seen brushing down an exhaust tube when Dorothy appears driving one of Malcolm's racing cars.

Leo looks up and places the exhaust upright against the garage wall. Dorothy pulls up and gets out of the car and Leo wipes his dirty hands on his overalls. "Dorothy, what's up?"
"Bad news I'm afraid, is my husband about?"

Dorothy hands Leo the telegram.
"He's busy in there as usual, got us all working around the clock on this new car." Leo starts reading the telegram and starts to look shocked as Dorothy did when she read it.
"I can't believe it, Malcolm's going to want to know about this, unbelievable, what a shame."
"I know; think of what poor Doris is going through, she must be in pieces poor women." They both go off inside the garage were the rest of the team are working on the new Bluebird which now has its wheels fitted to it.

Malcolm is sitting inside the new car while his mechanics are working on it. He sees Dorothy and Leo walking into the garage and climbs out of the Bluebird. "Hi honey, what do you think, we've almost finished her." says Malcolm looking confident.
"She looks great darling; I need you to read this, I'm afraid its bad news. "What is it? If it's a bill we will deal with it later as you can see we're far too busy." Malcolm looks preoccupied with the mechanics as Dorothy and Leo try to get his attention. "This is quite important boss, it's about Sir Henry and he's been killed!" The mechanics overhear the conversation and stop working as Malcolm walks closer towards Dorothy and Leo. "I beg your pardon, he's dead. How in god's name did that happen?" Replies Malcolm. Leo hands the telegram over to Malcolm and he starts reading it. "It says it was a boating accident while he was attempting the water speed record at Lake Windermere." Says Leo. All the mechanics looked shocked and gather around Malcolm. "What happened?" says one of the mechanics.
"He struck an object in the lake which killed him and his chief mechanic, what's so sad is he had already beating the water speed record and thought he could better it." Malcolm finishes reading the telegram. "If you could write a letter of condolences Dorothy, it's the least we can do."
Dorothy agrees nodding her head. "Of course." Dorothy leaves with Leo. Outside the garage Dorothy prepares to climb into the Austin car while Leo looks around it. Dorothy starts her up. "She sounds great Dorothy."
"Yes, she does, Leo promise me something; try to keep Malcolm save will you."
"I'll certainly try my best Dorothy."

Dorothy drives off and Leo heads back into the garage where
Inside Malcolm is standing to one side watching the mechanics working. Leo walks up to Malcolm.
"How is she?" says Malcolm. "She's worried, just as we all are."
"I keep telling her it'll be ok" says Malcolm.
They both walk towards the men working on the Bluebird.
One of the engine panels is open and Malcolm looks inside.
"You sure that engines going to be cool enough in there? "It looks awfully tight" says Malcolm. "It'll be fine; the radiator is doing its job."

DAYTONA BEACH. 5TH FEBRUARY 1931.

Hundreds of people are gathered around the new Bluebird with Malcolm and his team standing by it. The press can be seen talking to Malcolm and his team. "What speed are you hoping to achieve today Captain Campbell?" asks one of the reporters.
Malcolm looks confident and has his hands on his hips.
"We hope we can hit 250mph" says Malcolm. "We will keep our fingers crossed for you Captain, all the best."

The police start pushing the crowd back as the team start
to prepare the car for its run. Malcolm has all his gear on as he approaches the side of the Bluebird. Leo comes round to help Malcolm climb into the car.
As Malcolm climbs into the cockpit he pauses as Leo is seen wiping the sand off his shoes with a rag. Malcolm gets into the seat of the cockpit and checks his instruments and gives the signal to the team to start her up.
"Ok chaps, fire her up!"
A loud roar is heard as the engine comes to life with black smoke coming from the exhausts. Leo is seen running to the back of the car with the rest of the team as they prepare to push the car away. Malcolm selects 1st gear and gives the thumbs up to his team. The team push the car away and Malcolm heads off heading north up the beach. Faster and faster he goes as he flies through the measured mile.
A plane flies alongside him filming the attempt. The spectators are cheering. Malcolm slows the car down enough to turn it around and head back the other way down the beach.
He starts to pick up speed faster and faster and flies through the measured mile gripping the wheel tightly.
Suddenly the Bluebird pops out of gear and the gear lever smashes into Malcolm's leg. He fights to put it back into gear and carries on down the beach slowing the car down.
He heads towards his team who are waiting for him. Malcolm brings the car to a stop and his team run up to him as
Malcolm removes his goggles from his head. "Bloody gear lever smacked me in the leg Leo!"
Malcolm looks in pain as Leo helps him out of the car. "Are you alright boss?"
"I'll be fine, how did we do?"
The team look over and see one of the timing officials running over. "There you go gents, congratulations a new record."
One of Malcolm's team members reads the speed. "A speed of 246.09mph" shouts the team member. Everyone cheers while Malcolm smiles and looks to the ground. Leo pats Malcolm on the back. "It may not be 250mph but at least you've beating Segrave's record" says Leo. Malcolm smiles. "Yes and we will be back as I know she'll do more. Crowds start gathering around the team and the car.

Daytona Beach 1931

BROOKLANDS

Crowds gather to see the record breaking car.
Malcolm, his wife and his team are standing by the Bluebird.
Photographers can be seen taking photos.
In amongst the crowds of people is a woman dressed in a long fur coat wearing a hat. It is the late Sir Henry Segrave's wife Doris and she has come in person to see Malcolm's record breaking car. She

walks forward and Dorothy spots her and holds out both hands towards Doris who holds on to Dorothy's hands. "It's great to see you Doris, how are you keeping?" asks Dorothy. "I'm fine, thank you, congratulations by the way, you must be very proud of him."
"Yes, thank you." Replies Dorothy.
The team and Malcolm each bow their heads to Doris as she acknowledges them before she moves back into the crowd.
The press move forward to talk to Malcolm who's now leaning up against the car smoking a pipe.
"How's soon will you be returning back to Daytona as we hear you weren't entirely satisfied with the speed of the Bluebird?" asks the reporter. "That's right; I know the car can go much faster and we hope to take her back early next year after we've done some modifications. "Thank you Sir, we look forward to that."
"Now as I've arranged I'm going to be doing a parade lap around the circuit so give us some room please, thank you."
The team clear a path and push the Bluebird onto the track.
The Bluebird is started up and Malcolm drives it around the Brooklands circuit.

DAYTONA TOWN 24TH FEBRUARY 1932

A year has passed and Malcolm and his team are back in Daytona trying to increase the speed record. The team are being escorted through the town of Daytona with the new modified Bluebird car being towed by a truck. The Bluebird has its chrome discs removed from the wheels.

DAYTONA NIGHT CLUB

Flapper girls are up on stage performing wearing short frocks and wearing hats with large feathers in them.
They are tables in the club with people sitting at them with drinks on them. Malcolm and his team are seen sitting at one of the tables with drinks and watching the dancers performing.
"It's great in here boss."
"Yes, just don't tell the wife."
Malcolm and the others laugh while the dancers are still on stage doing there dance routine in time with the band that's playing.

BROOKLANDS JANUARY 1933

The team are all inside Thomson & Taylors garage when the phone rings. It's the engine company, Rolls Royce and they want to speak to Malcolm.
Malcolm goes to answer the phone in the office and shuts the door with the team outside the office looking on.

A few minutes later Malcolm comes back out of the office and walks up to the team. "That was Rolls Royce and there giving us an engine. It's an R type Sprint engine developing about 2500hp." Says Malcolm. "That's splendid, when does it arrive?" Asks Leo. "They said next week and it's a secret." The team look at one another.
Malcolm walks up to Leo and puts his hand on his shoulder.
"We're going to have to modify the chassis to take the weight and the size Leo." Leo nods his head "Sure thing boss."
Malcolm looks at the rest of the team. This engine we're getting is top secret and we're not to tell anyone outside this garage. Is that clear? Says Malcolm. The team nod and start discussing with Leo about modifying the chassis.

BROOKLANDS TRACK

Several weeks have passed and on Brooklands racetrack there is
a Sunbeam Tiger racing car being driven around the track by
Dorothy Campbell. In the paddock area are men standing in a line outside the Thomson & Taylors garage.
From inside the garage the modified Bluebird with the secret new Rolls Royce engine is being pushed out by Leo and
the team.

The Bluebird has no body panels fitted to it yet because they are still being made at Gurney & Nutting Ltd. Malcolm is standing off to one side. Malcolm climbs into the car and makes himself comfortable as the team look over the car. "How does it feel?" Asks Reid. Malcolm is holding the steering wheel. "Yes, it feels fine." Malcolm gets out of the car.
"Sure the radiator is going to be big enough to keep her cool?"
"We've made some modifications but I'm sure she's going to cope." Says Leo. Malcolm nods his head. "That's good, very good, well done chaps, good job."
Dorothy suddenly appears driving the Sunbeam racing car and
Malcolm walks up to the side of her as Dorothy switches the
engine off. "So what do you think Dorothy?"

Dorothy takes off her racing cap. "Yes, it's a lot smoother than before. The steering wheel still shudders round the corners but apart from that it's fine."

Dorothy climbs out of the Sunbeam and straightens her overalls out and walks over to the Bluebird with her husband Malcolm.
How's it coming along?" asks Dorothy. "Well it's a big engine Rolls Royce have giving us that I was surprised it fitted so well to the chassis."
"It looks great dear." Says Dorothy.
They walk up to the team standing around the new Bluebird.
"How did you find the Sunbeam Dorothy?" Leo asks.
"Yes it's a good improvement from the last one." They all smile at Dorothy and continue looking over the new Bluebird.

POVEY CROSS DAY

Malcolm is at home in front of the garage with his wife who is standing next to the new Bluebird and their son is sitting in the cockpit. Leo is standing nearby when Malcolm walks up to him. "Well Leo, not long to go now, hopefully we can finally reach that 300 barrier."
"Let's hope so, I'm exhausted." Malcolm laughs.

DAYTONA BEACH 22 FEBRUARY 1933

The team are placing the wheels on the Bluebird while
Malcolm watches wearing his white overalls and his brown racing cap.
The crowd have now exceeded 140.000 and look on as the Bluebird team prepare the car for its run.
Malcolm climbs into the car with Leo wiping his shoes as he climbs in. They start the mighty Rolls Royce engine with the help of the gas starter and Malcolm puts the car into 1st gear and the team push him away.
Malcolm picks up speed heading in a northerly direction up the beach. The crowd are cheering.
Malcolm slows the car down and turns it around to go back the other way down the beach. He picks up speed.
An aircraft is flying alongside him filming the event.
Malcolm flies through the measured mile at about 274mph.
The crowd continue to cheer him on as he speeds past.
Malcolm gradually slows the car down and drives towards his team who are waiting in the distance.
Malcolm pulls up by his team and jumps out of the car to his pleased team.
"It's still not quick enough Leo."
"I can't understand it. It must be the traction. We need more grip." Says Leo. One of the timing officials walks over and hands a piece of paper to one of the team members.
"So what was it?" Asks Leo. The team member looks at the piece of paper while Malcolm takes his racing cap off and wipes his face. "A speed of 272mph" says the team member.
The team cheer while Malcolm looks to the ground and smiles with his hands on his hips clutching his cap and racing gloves.

SAVOY HOTEL LONDON

Malcolm, his wife, Leo and his team are all sitting around a table with glasses of wine and eating food. Malcolm leans over towards Leo. "Any ideas on how we're going to hit the big 300 mark old chum?"
"Don't worry about it boss, I've already been drawing up plans with Reid on what needs to be done, now your here to relax and enjoy yourself, orders from Dorothy, so shut it and it your carrots!"
Malcolm looks shocked as Leo smiles and tucks into his food. Dorothy glances across to Leo and smiles while Malcolm looks down at his plate of food looking dumbfounded.

THOMSON AND TAYLOR BROOKLANDS

The mechanics are busy working on a long chassis with double wheels and tyres fitted to the rear axle. The front of the car has a vent built around the radiator which can be opened and closed. Leo is talking to Reid Railton. "With the double wheels I reckon you should gain an extra 50mph." Leo nods. "I've suggested to Malcolm that we may need to consider finding another site that can give better traction, but he won't have it, not after the problems we had in Africa."
"That was a dried up lake pan wasn't it? Asks Reid.
"Yes it was and it gave us better traction." Replies Leo.
"Hopefully with this new setup we won't need to look elsewhere."
"I've got the coach builders, Gurney Nutting working on the body of the car, it should look great." Says Reid. They continue watching the team work on the new car which they are now calling the Bluebird 5.

UNVEILING OF THE BLUEBIRD 5

Several weeks have passed and a crowd of people and press have gathered outside the garage waiting for the new Bluebird to be unveiled. Malcolm appears from one of the garage side doors and addresses the press. "It gives me great pleasure ladies and gentlemen to introduce to you our new car Bluebird 5."
The crowd eagerly look on as the garage door opens and Malcolm's team roll out the car.

The Bluebird 5.

The crowd look amazed as photographers take photos.
It's a thing of beauty Sir." Malcolm smiles.
"Yes indeed she is and she'll be generating about 2300hp with her 36.7 litre engine." Replies Malcolm.
"When will you be making your next attempt Sir?" asks the reporter while Malcolm looks confident with his hands on his waist. "We should hope to be ready by early next year where we hope to break the 300mph barrier."
The crowd look amazed and talk amongst themselves while Malcolm leans up against the Bluebird with Leo wiping certain parts of the car with a rag while the press continue taking photographs.

DAYTONA BEACH 7TH MARCH 1935

Thousands of people line the beach.
The Bluebird team are preparing the car while Malcolm stands to one side and watches. Leo is helping change the wheels over from treaded to slicks. Malcolm is doing up his racing cap.
"Good to go boss? "Yes, let's go!" Leo helps Malcolm into the cockpit, wiping his shoes as he gets in. Leo goes to stand by the gas starter while the team look on ready to go. Malcolm is gripping the steering wheel with his head down in the cockpit.
Malcolm gives Leo the thumbs up to start.
Leo turns over the gas starter and it starts up the Rolls Royce engine with black smoke coming from the exhausts.
Malcolm puts it into first gear and the team push him away.
A plane can be seen flying alongside the Bluebird filming the attempt as the car goes faster and faster.

Suddenly Malcolm has a problem, his front right tyre starts shredding chunks of rubber everywhere and he is forced to slow down and stop the car. The team at the north end help Malcolm out of the car and set about changing the tyres.

The press start approaching Malcolm who is seen taking his cap off. Malcolm runs his hands through his hair while the team frantically get the car ready for its return run.

"Is everything ok Sir?" asks the reporter.

Malcolm picks up one of the wheels that have just come off the Bluebird. "As you can see Gentlemen the tyres have been shredded by the hard sand."

The press look on as the team work on preparing the car.

Leo is seen walking over to Malcolm looking concerned.

"We can't keep this up Boss. We need more grip. We must consider looking for another salt lake like the one in Africa. "The beach is just not giving us the grip we need."

Malcolm looks exhausted and frustrated.

"You've been talking to that bloke about the dried up lake in Utah?" Leo looks to the ground and shakes his head in frustration. "It just makes sense."

One of the officials runs over to Malcolm and his team.

"You have 15 mins left gentlemen" says the official.

The team hurry while Malcolm puts his cap back on.

"Ok Leo, let's see how we do on this run, if it's no good we'll go to Utah agreed?"

"Agreed!" The team close all the engine panels down tight and Malcolm climbs into the car. Leo runs to the side of the car where the gas starter is attached to the engine with hoses and he prepares to start it up. Malcolm makes one final check of his instruments and puts his thumb up to Leo while the rest of the team are behind the Bluebird ready to push her away.

"Go on then Leo; let's start her up, on three, one two three contact!" The mighty Rolls Royce engine kicks into life bellowing black smoke out of the exhausts and Leo removes the hosing from the engine compartment and closes the engine cover. The team push Malcolm away as Malcolm puts it into gear.

BONNEVILLE SALT FLATS UTAH 3rd SEPTEMBER 1935

Leo and Malcolm's son Donald are in the Lincoln car chasing Malcolm's Bluebird along the salt flats.

"Come on Leo, faster!"

"This is as fast as she will go Donald."

Donald leans forward and places his hands on the car's dashboard and looks through the window.

"I can't see him Leo, Dads too far ahead."

They continue chasing the Bluebird. Malcolm is speeding across the salt flats at about 290mph.

Malcolm is seen gripping the steering wheel hard as he tries to keep the car in a straight line as white dust flies up around the car when suddenly his front left tyre blows and causes the car to spin sideways.

Malcolm manages to get the car under control and brings it to a stop. With his hands shaking he raises his goggles and climbs out of the car.

With smoke coming from the damaged wheel he steps back from the car and looks along the whole length of the car with his hands on his head still shaking.

In the distance Malcolm can see an approaching car.

Donald and Leo can see the smoke coming from the front of the Bluebird with Malcolm resting up against the side of her.

"What do you think has happened Leo? Is father ok?"

Leo looks across looking concerned as he drives up to the Bluebird. "He looks ok, let's find out" says Leo.
They both get out of the Lincoln car and run over.
"Donald, don't touch the Bluebird as it will be hot!" Donald runs up to his dad and gives him a hug.
"What happened father?"
"The tyre burst my son but we'll get it fixed."
Leo walks up to the burst tyre on the Bluebird and then looks at Malcolm. "Yes Leo I know, just check it hasn't damaged the axle, where are the others?"
"They won't be long" says Leo while a plane flies overhead.
The rest of the team turn up with all the spares and fresh tyres and start on getting the tyres changed.
Dorothy can be seen getting out of a car and walks over.
Malcolm sees Dorothy walking over.
"Leo, I don't want Dorothy seeing the state of the tyre."
Leo covers the damaged tyre. Dorothy walks up to Malcolm who is standing with Donald. "Everything go alright?" Malcolm smiles. "Yes, great dear." Dorothy nods and smiles.
"Well just go careful and I'll see you at the other end."

She kisses him on the cheek while Malcolm looks over to Leo who is sitting on the blown tyre that's covered up.
Malcolm walks over to Leo while Dorothy gets into a car.
"Well that was close; do you think she would of let you continue if she saw this?"
"I don't know Leo; let's just get the car ready for the return run."
"Ok boss." replies Leo
Malcolm prepares himself to get back in the Bluebird while the team put new wheels and tyres on.
Malcolm watches as his wife drives off with the others back to the start point. Malcolm looks at Leo.
"We good to go Leo?"
Leo is seen with the team doing up the last wheel nuts on the Bluebird. "Yep, give us a few more seconds."
Malcolm climbs into the Bluebird and puts on his gloves.
Leo clears the team away from the car and prepares to start its engine with the gas starter.
Leo looks at Malcolm. "Ready!"
"Go on. And contact" says Malcolm.
The engine roars into life while Leo removes the gas starters hosing. The team push the car away and Malcolm puts it into first gear and he's away.
Malcolm is seen accelerating away faster and faster off into the distance. Donald goes to climb into the car.
"Come on Leo, Dad's getting away!"
"Ok, I'm coming."
Leo passes the Bluebird's engine starter to the team members to put on the back of a truck. Leo then heads to Donald who's waiting by the car. They both get in the Lincoln car and drive off after the Bluebird that's disappeared off into the distance.

TIMING TOWER

The timing officials can see Malcolm approaching in the Bluebird at high speed. "Here he comes! "I think I've got a problem with the timing instruments."
One of the officials looks over at the other.

"What do you mean? We can't ask them to do another run, get it sorted." Both officials frantically try to calculate the timings as the Bluebird flies through the measured mile markers. Malcolm Campbell deploys the windbreaks which are located at the rear of the Bluebird to help slow her down.

Malcolm drives the Bluebird towards the timing tower and brings it to a stop. Malcolm climbs out of it.
The Bluebird is smoking as Malcolm rests up against it still wearing his racing cap and looking pleased with his run. Dorothy and some of the Bluebird team arrive at the timing tower and walk over towards Malcolm and the team to start checking the Bluebird over.

Dorothy walks over to Malcolm and kisses him on the cheek.
"Have you got the timings yet?"
"No not yet." Malcolm looks over at the officials as Leo, Donald and the rest of the team turn up in their vehicles.
Leo and Donald get out of the Lincoln car and Donald runs over to his Dad and gives him a hug. Leo walks over to Malcolm.
"All good Boss?"
"Yes Leo, but I think the timing officials have a problem.
We can't run the Bluebird again, we don't have the tyres."
Malcolm and the team look concerned as one of the official's walks over. "We are sorry for the delay Sir, but we're having problems with the instruments." Malcolm looks at Leo as the team continue going over the Bluebird whilst they wait for the timings. One of the officials runs over.
"Sorry for the delay, our calculations were wrong."
Leo takes the piece of paper off the official and reads it.
"We've done it a speed of 301.13mph." Everyone starts cheering and clapping.

The 20s and 30s will always be known as the golden age of land speed record breaking.

An era where men pushed themselves to the limits of their abilities to become the fastest men on land or in Malcolm Campbell's case a speed king.

THE END

Kind regards

To

Don Wales & family.

Printed in Great Britain
by Amazon